Trade Press

Advertising, Marketing and PR

The Insider Career Guides *is a dynamic series of books designed to give you the inside track on individual careers – how to get in, how to get on, even how to get out.*

Based on the real-life experiences of people actually working in these fields, each title offers a combination of hard practical information and insider information on working culture, the pros and cons of different areas of work, prospects for promotion, etc.

Other titles in the series:

Banking and the City
Karen Holmes

Broadcasting and the Media
Paul Redstone

The Environment
Melanie Allen

Information and Communications Technology
Jacquetta Megarry

Retailing
Liz Edwards

Sport
Robin Hardwick

Travel and Tourism
Karen France

About the Series Editor

Following a successful career as a teacher and lecturer in the UK and the Far East, Karen Holmes now works as a freelance writer, editor and project manager. Specialising in learning and careers, she has authored a range of careers literature for publishers and other commercial organisations.

Advertising, Marketing and PR

by

Karen Holmes

First published in 2000 by
The Industrial Society
Robert Hyde House
48 Bryanston Square
London W1H 7LN

ISBN 1 85835 872 8

British Library Cataloguing-in-Publication Data.
A catalogue record for this book is available from the British Library.

Typeset by: The Midlands Book Typesetting Company
Printed by: Cromwell Press
Cover by: Sign Design
Cover image by: Roy Botterell

The Industrial Society is a Registered Charity No. 290003

CONTENTS

INTRODUCTION

> A man had a dream. In the dream, St. Peter came to him and said, 'When you die, you can go either to heaven or to hell.'
> He showed the man heaven. It was like an expensive nightclub, full of beautiful people sipping Champagne. Then he showed the man hell, a dark pit with no air conditioning and a demon throwing people into a huge fire.
> 'If you want to go to heaven,' St. Peter said, 'you need to mend your ways.'
> The man mended his ways, lived a boring but exemplary life and died when he was 60. He went straight up the celestial escalator and met St. Peter outside the pearly gates.
> 'So,' said St. Peter, 'let's check your record. Yes, you cleaned up your act. It's heaven for you. Step inside.'
> He opened the gate and the man went in. He was back in that dark smoky pit and the demon was waving his pitchfork.
> 'Hey, wait!' the man cried. 'What happened to the beautiful people and the Champagne?'
> 'Oh that,' St. Peter said, 'that was just our marketing department.'

Are you thinking about a career in advertising, marketing or public relations? Perhaps you see yourself in a creative role, developing concepts and coming up with the visuals or words that make products sell. Maybe you are searching for an opening into the marketing function of a large organisation or thinking about setting up your own PR agency. You could simply be curious to know whether the world of advertising, marketing and PR is as glamorous as it's made out to be. Whatever your interest, you'll find information and answers to your questions in this book.

When you start to think about your future and consider a particular career, you need to carry out some research to discover what opportunities are available to you. You will need to contact organisations that offer relevant training and qualifications, look at recruitment literature and study advertisements to get a clearer idea of the current state of the job market. Above all, you'll need to talk to the professionals, the people who already work in your chosen field. That is the only way you will get a realistic view of the career you plan to follow.

In these *Insider Career Guides*, we have done some of the hard work for you by researching specific career areas and talking to people who work in them. Consequently, we can give you the inside story about different professions and their cultures, day-to-day working routines and the opportunities that exist for you.

In this book, *The Insider Career Guide to Advertising, Marketing and PR,* you will find useful information about:

- starting your career
- the qualities employers look for in their new recruits
- the pay and benefits you can expect
- opportunities for training and development
- promotion and getting ahead
- planning your job search.

The book is divided into three sections; *The Job, The Person* and *Getting in, Getting on... Getting out,* followed by an all-important *Jargon buster* to help you negotiate the 'language' of advertising, marketing and PR.

Part One, *The Job,* looks at the differences (and similarities) between advertising, marketing and PR. It will give you an up-to-date overview of all three areas of employment, including:

- trends in recruitment
- different types of jobs in each sector
- salaries, perks and holidays
- working conditions
- office 'culture'
- contract work and freelancing.

Part Two, *The Person,* focuses on the people who work in these industries. It will help you to think about:

- what you want from your job
- why you've chosen this career field
- what employers want from you
- the skills and qualities that contribute to success.

Part Three, *Getting in, Getting on... Getting out,* considers:

- opportunities for college leavers, graduates and mature entrants
- study options related to advertising, marketing and PR
- how to find out about vacancies and apply for them
- how to succeed at an interview or assessment centre
- how to seize opportunities for promotion.

And finally, should you ever feel that you want to move on, this *Insider Career Guide* considers how you can get out of the industry and into a new career, or start to work for yourself.

You can't expect any book to answer all your questions, so in the final pages there is a list of contact and website addresses that will help you to continue your research.

With case studies, quotes from insiders and 'myth busters' that address common misconceptions about advertising, marketing and PR, you should find plenty of inside information in these pages to help you start your chosen career.

part one the job

the job

Introduction

Get a job in advertising, marketing or PR and life will be one big party. Your capacity to drink Champagne and the quality of your wardrobe will be as important as your talent. You won't have to go into the office unless you want to, and you'll never have to wear a suit. You will be out on the town every night, you'll mix with the rich and famous (isn't there a member of the royal family in PR?) – and we haven't even begun to mention the freebies and the exotic location shoots...

In fact, you'll get to do everything a hedonist could ever dream of, and you'll get to call it work...

We wish. Edina may have put over an 'absolutely fabulous' image of working in the fast lane of PR, and there may have been a smidgen of truth lurking beneath the laughs, but the reality is that, for most people who work in advertising, marketing and PR, stress and hard slog are more likely to typify your days rather than Bollinger for breakfast and lunch at Harvey Nicks.

These are some of the most competitive career areas for job seekers. You will fight to get in, you will fight to get to the top and then you will fight to stay there. All that fighting doesn't leave a lot of time for anything else. Luckily, most people who are employed in these fields love their work, so the demands on their time and energy are sources of pleasure rather than a burden.

This book looks at careers in three industries. Advertising, marketing and PR are related but they are not the same. They each have a different focus and they each involve different skills. Some people may move from marketing into PR or vice versa, but there are distinctions between the three career areas and you need to be clear on what these are.

The common feature of all three (and the reason we have grouped them together in one book) is that they are part of the communications industry. Whether you are selling a product, preparing a political press release or launching a new restaurant, you are communicating a message and influencing the way the public think. That can give you enormous power.

Another reason for looking at these areas collectively is that there is a lot of crossover between them. Many people move from advertising into a marketing or PR function and vice versa. Some agencies will service all their clients' communications needs, including advising them on marketing strategy, preparing sales and promotional material and advertisements, and staging exhibitions and special events. Larger agencies may well have a number of divisions, such as an advertising agency, direct marketing agency and sales promotions section, under one roof.

In the first part of this *Insider Career Guide,* we are going to examine what opportunities and types of jobs exist in advertising, marketing and PR.

ADVERTISING

> 'Advertising is the greatest art form of the 20th century.'
>
> *Marshall McLuhan, Canadian communications guru*
>
> 'Advertising may be described as the science of arresting human intelligence long enough to get money from it.'
>
> *Stephen Leacock, Canadian political scientist and humorist*

Advertising has given us some of the most enduring images and phrases of our age. Advertisements stimulate debate and sometimes controversy. They make us laugh and they can reduce us to tears. They have a powerful effect on the human consciousness because they are all around us, on television, radio, in cinemas, newspapers and magazines.

Advertisements make us part with our money or pledge our allegiance. Ultimately, advertising is about manipulating public opinion and getting a message across to an audience so that they will behave in a particular way. Whether that involves buying a particular brand of teabag or supporting a charity, effective advertisements will ensure that we react in the required manner.

The history of advertising

Prostitution and spying are reputed to be the world's oldest professions, but advertising may be still older. In its most basic form, advertising is something we are all involved in all the time. The way that we dress, talk and behave sends a message to other people. We promote ourselves by the image we present, in just the same way that an advertising agency promotes a client's product.

The advertising industry has been in existence since the end of the 17th century, when newsheets carried printed advertisements for products and information. Merchants returning from voyages overseas needed to generate markets for the products they imported – so they advertised. Early advertisements may have been fairly simple in style, but they did show many of the characteristics of their modern descendants in that they attempted to deliver information economically and in a visually arresting way.

By the end of the 19th century, advertising was big business. Agencies, whose primary function was to create and disseminate advertisements on behalf of client companies, sprang up. Newspapers, realising what a money-spinner advertising could be, dedicated more space to display ads. As newspaper circulation grew and literacy levels improved, the potential for reaching large audiences with news of products and services was enormous.

The new science of psychology enabled practitioners to explore what stimulated a response in audiences, thus making the whole process more sophisticated. This hastened the move away from information-led to image-led advertisements, where a single picture could be used to tell a story or communicate a complex message.

Advertisements rapidly began to dominate newspapers and the increasingly popular women's magazines. Posters were commonplace and spawned a whole art form. But it was a new communication technology that gave the industry its biggest boost. Television advertising came to Britain in

1955, when advertisers were given the chance to buy time on the commercial, independent television stations.

Modern advertising exploits every medium of communication. We tend to think of ads in terms of the 'mainstream media', such as television, radio, newspaper and magazines, but other methods are increasingly being used to 'spread the word'. Posters and billboards, point-of-sale displays, direct selling and cold-calling by phone and fax are all readily accessible for the advertisers. Teletext services are used to send information and advertisements into any home that has a compatible television set.

Perhaps the biggest development in recent years is the expansion of advertising on the Internet. This has massive potential in that it taps into worldwide audiences; it offers new fields for creativity and a facility for direct response from those who see the ads – and it is very hard to ignore.

Whatever your attitude towards advertising, you cannot deny its influence. The slogans, the music, the images and the logos are part of our consciousness and our culture. If you work in advertising, you will be part of an influential band of people who can really change public attitudes and behaviour.

The advertising industry

In terms of the number of people it employs, advertising is not a massive industry in the UK. In 1999, the Advertising Association estimated that fewer than 20,000 people were employed by agencies in this country. Nevertheless, it is a multi-billion pound industry, a fact that is testimony to how much money organisations are willing to pay to get their messages across. In 1998, more than £14.31 billion was spent on advertising in the UK: £3 billion of that was spent on television advertising alone.[1]

Because it is a relatively small industry (but one with a very high profile), competition for vacancies is fierce. Figures vary, but the following statistics give some idea of what a job seeker is up against:

---

[1] *BRAD*, EMAP Business Communications, page 21, September 1999

- graduate applications exceed vacancies b,
- fewer than 50 agencies have formal grau... recruitment programmes
- high-profile agencies may receive more than 2,000 applications for a single advertised vacancy.

If you are committed to starting a career in advertising, you will not allow these statistics to put you off. Yes, it is hard to get in, but plenty of people do succeed.

Advertising agencies

The heart of the industry lies in the advertising agencies. Their size and scope vary enormously. The smallest agencies may have only three or four permanent staff and access to freelancers for specialist help, such as copywriting or media buying. The large agencies are multinationals with offices in such far-flung places as Beijing and Buenos Aires. But even they are not massive employers; few of the big-name agencies employ more than 300 staff in their offices in this country.

- McCann Erickson Advertising Ltd. is the largest advertising agency in the world, with a presence in 110 countries and a client list that includes Nestlé, Unilever, Boots and AT&T. It employs 300 people at its office in the West End of London.
- Leo Burnett has won dozens of awards worldwide and handles many of the world's top brands. It has 320 staff working from its London office.
- Abbott Mead Vickers BBDO is the biggest agency in the UK and handles clients such as BT, Guinness, Wrangler and Sainsbury's. It has 321 staff in London.

Other familiar names include Saatchi and Saatchi, J. Walter Thompson and Ogilvy and Mather. For up-to-date information on agencies and the types of accounts they handle, check out the *Advertisers Annual* or the *Standard Directory of International Advertisers and Agencies*. See *Want to read all about it?* at the end of this book for details.

> 'London is still the hub of the advertising industry – that's where most of the money is spent and the vast majority of agencies are located. There are advertising and marketing communities in other cities around the country such as Manchester, Leeds and Edinburgh, and you'll find small agencies and consultancies in almost every town, although many of these will work primarily with local clients and media.'
>
> *Agency partner*

If you work in a small agency, you may be expected to do everything, including account management, client liaison, concept development, creative work and making the tea. In a larger agency, job roles will be more structured. You will have a specific role and a greater chance of more formal career development. It is horses for courses; some people love the involvement and buzz of doing everything themselves, others prefer to work in a company which has a more defined organisational structure.

> 'One major decision everybody should make before they start applying for jobs is whether they want to work for a large or small company. Working in a small agency is much more a case of rolling up your sleeves and mucking in, and it's a 360-degree experience. In a big agency, you'll be involved more in delegation and management – it can be a bit of a conveyor belt. But if you serve your apprenticeship in one of the blue-chip companies, you'll have big-name connections and that can pave your way later.'
>
> *New business director, communications agency*

Advertising agencies vary in the services they offer. The most familiar names are full-service agencies, but there are other successful companies that specialise in media services or focus on particular areas of advertising, such as recruitment or business-to-business advertising.

Full-service agencies

Imagine that you are a manufacturer. You have developed a new product – let's say it's a new type of screwdriver – that you think will revolutionise the DIY market. You want to promote your product on the open market but you know nothing about advertising and have no desire to direct your own campaign. What do you do? You go to a full-service agency that can offer a comprehensive service to plan your advertising campaign, design and produce it and deliver it to selected media.

If this is done well it is not a simple process. Those snappy slogans and persistent images with which we are so familiar are as likely to be the result of thorough research and planning as a flash of inspiration.

Advertising campaigns bring together the aspirations of the client with the needs and desires of the target audience. They have to be effective because they cost a lot of money. They have to comply with the standards set by regulatory bodies such as the Advertising Standards Association and the Independent Television Commission. They have to tap into the modern psyche.

To ensure that all these needs are met, agency staff will spend a great deal of time researching prospective customers to find out what catches their eye, what makes them buy and what keeps them buying. Questions will also be asked about timing (to establish the optimum time to launch a campaign) and about budgets. At the same time, there will be close liaison with the client to ensure that their expectations are being met.

So, 'campaign' is not a word that is used lightly. An advertising campaign can have all the features of a military operation.

Once ideas for the campaign begin to take shape, 'creatives' will add their special talents to put concepts into images and words. At the same time, media planners and buyers will be identifying suitable channels through which to present the advertisements so as to get maximum market penetration. They may be buying space in newspapers and magazines, or airtime on TV and radio, or tying up deals to put advertisements on the Internet.

The production team will take the advertising concept to its final stage. That may be finished artwork and photography for a print ad, or shooting a video for a television ad or a combination of different components for a variety of media.

The advertisements will be released, hopefully at a time when they will gain maximum attention. The campaign launch is not the end of the story, however. Agencies will constantly monitor the success of their production to make sure it delivers results. Agencies cannot afford to be complacent; if a client is unhappy with a campaign and takes their custom elsewhere, it could cost the agency millions of pounds in turnover and ruin their reputation.

Agencies earn their money either by charging fees or by taking a percentage of the amount they spend on behalf of their clients. For example, if a client has £5 million to invest in a product launch, the agency may take 15% of that amount.

> 'Commercially, we have to deliver the financial targets that have been set for us by senior management within the agency – we have to get the turnover and the profit. We're running a business here and we can't afford to produce a campaign, however brilliant, that doesn't come within our client's budget. If we overspend, we'd end up paying for it ourselves.'
>
> *Account manager*

As we have already said, some advertising agencies focus on particular areas, such as recruitment, business-to-business or financial services advertising, that demand specialist creative and media planning skills. Their teams have the advantage of being familiar with the market in which they work – something that can be particularly useful in some technical and industrial fields.

Media specialist agencies

Also known as media independents, these agencies concentrate on research, media planning and buying, using their specialist knowledge to place ads in the appropriate media at the right cost. Some clients will divide a job between two agencies, using one advertising company to produce the campaign and a media specialist to place it. Although the larger full-service agencies will have media departments to take care of this function, smaller advertising agencies will use the services of media specialists if they do not have the expertise in-house.

Direct mail

An estimated 2.8 billion items of direct mail are put out in this country every year. That figure represents a lot of business – and profit – for companies that work in this field.

Direct mail agencies may combine both marketing and advertising expertise. They create ads that go direct to the customer by post, fax or Internet. Direct mail agencies usually offer the same services as full-service agencies, including account planning and management, creative work and production. They may organise despatch themselves or use separate companies to send out printed material to potential customers. In the computer age, targeting direct mail is an exact science involving database management, an understanding of purchasing patterns and an ability to analyse vast amounts of research material.

New media

New media, particularly the growth of Internet advertising, is taking the industry by storm. Between 1997 and 1998, UK Internet advertising revenue grew by 138% to nearly £20 million.[2] Although that is just a fraction of the total yearly spend on advertising, it marks a significant increase for a medium of communication that has only been around for the last five years.

As millions of people connect on line every week, Internet advertising offers a personalised form of contact. Ads are placed right in people's homes where they cannot be missed. Customers have the option of responding immediately – and that is a powerful tool when you want somebody to part with their money. Advertisers can track the success of their ads by monitoring the number of hits (that means the number of times Internet users access their sites) and

[2] *The Daily Telegraph,* 11 September 1999

can also tap into valuable customer information and databases. Via e-mail, they can register customers' needs and build close customer relationships.

Increasingly sophisticated software means that advertisers can combine graphics, text and sound to create impact and spread their message. With 320 million pages on the Web (and by the time you read this, that figure will have significantly increased), most of which have the potential to carry some form of advertising, it does not take a mathematical genius to work out how powerful Internet advertising has become.

Full-service agencies are well aware of the growth of new media and many have established departments that can offer this service. There is also an increasing number of specialist companies across the country that deal exclusively in new media advertising.

> 'Companies have to exploit new media. We have to keep up with new technology and look for innovation. That can be hard when you are under pressure to keep up with the day-to-day work, but we can't afford to be left behind. We're constantly looking for new slants on things you've seen before.'
>
> *Creative services manager, advertising agency*

JOBS IN ADVERTISING

After that whistle-stop tour of different types of advertising companies, we can look in more detail at some of the jobs available within agencies. As we have already indicated, staff in small agencies will be multi-functional, but in larger agencies will probably work in one of the following areas:

- management
- planning
- creative
- production.

These are dealt with in some detail on the following pages because similar roles exist in many marketing and PR agencies.

Management

Account managers (who, depending on their level of seniority and the agency in which they work, may also be known as account handlers or account directors) liaise with the client. It is their job to know the client, to identify their aims and to understand the industry in which the client operates. This knowledge is used to brief the creative, planning and production teams so that they can develop appropriate advertisements. This is a job that demands advanced communication and organisational skills. As an account manager, you may be dealing with people from very different backgrounds whose ideas do not always coincide. You also have to deliver the finished product on time and within budget.

Planning

In some agencies, the same person will carry out management and planning. In larger agencies, there may well be a planning function responsible for research into both customer preferences and media positioning.

Research is used to determine audience perceptions. This is a vital step in placing products, services and information in such a way that they 'sell'. With such a proliferation of advertising in everyday life, audiences can become immune to its influence. Planners help to target campaigns so that this doesn't happen.

Research may be carried out in-house or passed on to independent market research companies. Through surveys, focus groups and statistical analysis planners will develop a strategy that places advertising in the right media at the right time. The findings of media planners may also influence the region in which a television commercial is broadcast and the time that it goes out, the location of a billboard campaign or the decision to place advertising on the Internet.

Media buyers negotiate with the media owners (newspapers, magazines, television companies, display companies, etc.) to buy space and time at the right cost. This demands a thorough knowledge of the media and the ability to negotiate, sometimes at a very high level. With the proliferation of new media, including cable and satellite television and the Internet, the media planner and buyer's job has become more complex – but also more challenging.

Creative

The lure of working as a creative remains undimmed. Creatives are often seen as the 'personalities' of an agency. Those few copywriters and designers who create truly successful advertising campaigns can achieve celebrity status.

Copywriters work closely with designers to produce the words that complement the images within an advertisement. Copywriters and designers often form permanent teams and work exclusively together, moving as a unit from one agency to the next.

> 'As a copywriter, you may be producing anything from slogans and strap lines to sell baked beans to specialist technical copy about computer hardware. It is not an easy job. The need to be "creative" day in and day out can be draining, and there is constant pressure to be innovative and find new ways to express familiar concepts. It is also a highly competitive field. Many people are aware that they have no artistic talent and would never aspire to be designers but everyone can write, can't they? Anyone can come up with a good turn of phrase. As a copywriter, you will continually be fighting other people's expectations.'
>
> *Freelance copywriter*

The terminology for the 'picture people' can be rather confusing. A creative director will develop the visual element of an advertisement. A visualiser will put those ideas on to paper. Their brief is to produce rough designs and layouts that will be developed into finished artwork, using a combination of drawing, photography and typography. Then there is the art director who will usually work with photographers and direct photo shoots to create the required images.

Computer technology has revolutionised the design process and visualisers may spend more time at a computer screen than a drawing board. Producing finished artwork is a skilled and specialist job – you may see vacancies for these positions under the heading 'Mac operator'. However, for creative directors and visualisers, talent and appropriate training in graphic arts or design remain essential.

Like copywriting, this is a demanding job. You need both talent and discipline to carry ideas through. In a small agency, the same person may be responsible for the whole development and production process. In larger agencies, the creative director will develop the ideas but may use specialist finished artists to put the final package together.

Production

The term 'creative services' is frequently used to refer to the production department. Depending on the type of advertising you work in, this can cover everything from overseeing the production of television and radio commercials to supervising print. Production demands staff with specialist skills and it offers good openings for people with the right background and training.

> 'I manage a team of five staff. A lot of my work involves planning and scheduling work so that jobs are completed on time, so I'm liaising with both staff in the agency and people outside such as printers. My background is varied – I did commercial studies at A level, worked for a photographer and a repro house and got a lot of job-based training. I learned about production and print by working with it. When we get new staff in the department, I always try to get them on to specific projects straightaway. It may be looking after a client's stationery, organising the image library or researching new technologies that we might want to use.'
>
> *Creative services manager, advertising agency*

Advertising sales

If you want to break in to advertising, then you may find a way in through advertising sales. This is not the glamour end of the market but, nevertheless, it is an area where vacancies may be easier to find and where you can learn the basics about the industry.

Advertising sales staff sell space for newspapers and magazines, and airtime for commercial broadcasting companies. They may be dealing with clients who regularly require roughly the same amount of space, or cold calling to sell space for a new publication or advertising outlet.

Most people in advertising sales will work on the phone at first and rarely get out of the office. This is a job that demands a lot of confidence, persistence and the ability to sell. Work is target-driven and salaries are based on achieving specified goals. Experienced staff can move rapidly through the ranks to become team leaders and to eventually dealing face to face with their own special group of clients.

MYTH BUSTER

There's never a dull moment if you work in advertising

Every job has its dull moments. It doesn't matter whether you are a world-famous film star, a space scientist or the chairman of London's flavour-of-the-month ad agency, there will still be elements of routine in your working day. Yes, advertising can be great fun and sometimes very exciting — but not all of the time.

'Why are people attracted to advertising? It still has an image of glamour, of being more informal than a lot of industries. Having said that, a lot of young people, particularly those who haven't worked before, have very unrealistic expectations about working in advertising. They think that's it's hyper-informal and that, from day one, they'll be involved in creating multi-million pound television campaigns with highly creative people. They don't anticipate the routine and the drudgery – and, of course, you get that in advertising just as you do in any other line of work.'

Agency partner, advertising agency

MARKETING

The *International Dictionary of Management* defines marketing as follows:

> 'A creative management function which promotes business and employment by assessing needs of the end user of products or services, initiates research and development, and produces products or services which can be profitably provided to service market requirements. It co-ordinates the resources of production and distribution of goods and services, determines and directs the nature and scale of the total effort required to sell profitably the maximum production to the ultimate user.'[3]

In simple English, that means ensuring customers get what they want, when they want it! Good marketing can persuade people they want or need something and can create demand. No product or service can be sold to the public without being marketed in some shape or form.

Marketing is customer rather than product focused. That means understanding how everything about your product or service impinges on the customer. It's not just the product itself that counts, but the way in which it is presented, delivered, repaired and replaced. If you want to breed customer loyalty then you have to look at the big picture.

If you are planning to work in marketing, you will have to get used to analysing products and services to find out their market position. A loaf of bread will never be the same again because every time you look at it, you'll be asking:

- who is the customer for this type of bread?
- what benefits does it offer that other loaves do not?
- why is it unlike other makes of bread?
- what image does the presentation of this loaf suggest?
- how can we persuade customers that they need this type of bread?

... and so on and so forth.

---

[3] Hans Johannsen and G. Terry Page, *International Dictionary of Management*, Kogan Page, 1996

In an increasingly crowded marketplace, the image of a product and the way in which it is branded are crucial to its success. Consequently, manufacturers will invest a great deal of money to differentiate their products from the competition.

Choosing a name can cost anything from £15,000 for a choice of three possible names for the domestic market, to around £100,000 if the product is being distributed on the international market. The name will establish the identity of the product and help the manufacturer to protect their trademark. In theory, paying such a large amount will also prevent the manufacturer from making an unfortunate name choice that could make its products the butt of cultural and linguistic jokes. Swedish toilet paper called Krapp, and the car name Nova that translates from Spanish to English as 'no go', are notable examples of what can happen if a product name is not chosen carefully.

To give a product an identity within the market can cost hundreds of thousands of pounds, but it is worth it if the brand is successfully established. A brand name and image can endure for a very long time, despite changes in advertising campaigns.

Evidence of this comes in the shape of products that we associate with their brand name. We don't drink cola, we drink Coke. If you buy a pair of Levi's, you don't need to explain to anybody that you are buying denim jeans. And how many of you use the phrase, 'going for a McDonald's'?

The power of marketing should not be underestimated. Research has shown that brand awareness kicks into a child's psyche when they are as young as 18 months-old. As we grow up, it defines our ideas of what products are acceptable and how they can help us belong to our society.

Small wonder, then, that many consultancies have been established to specialise in aspects of marketing. These range from full-service agencies, which will guide manufacturers and service providers through the whole marketing process, to specialist agencies that concentrate on one aspect of the marketing mix, such as researching names.

All manufacturers and service providers have marketing

departments. These are central to the rest of the company's operations. Marketing touches on many areas of product management; the marketing department will be involved from the very beginning of a product's life in determining its image, deciding when, where and how it should be launched, and monitoring its success in the marketplace. Marketing staff may also work on rebranding a product if it starts to lose popularity, or launching the product into new markets overseas.

JOBS IN MARKETING

Look at the appointments section of any broadsheet newspaper and you will find plenty of advertisements for marketing assistants, managers and directors. Marketing offers a range of career opportunities at different levels for people who are interested in making things sell.

In a large organisation, the marketing function will work in tandem with other functions, such as buying, logistics, distribution and retailing. If this is your chosen field, you will be working at the heart of your company and will gain valuable experience in many different aspects of management.

> 'Our marketing campaigns allow us to penetrate new areas and to talk to potential customers. A good marketing campaign delivers a professional image of the business and paves the way for our sales team to make a direct approach.'
>
> *Marketing manager, distribution company*

Openings may exist for school and college leavers as marketing assistants, and for graduates as trainee marketing managers. To beat the competition in getting these jobs, it is useful to have some relevant sales or marketing experience. You will be more interesting to prospective employers if you can show an interest in, and awareness of, consumer psychology even if this is only through part-time work in your local supermarket.

Another good source of marketing vacancies is the

independent marketing agencies and consultancies. These vary in size, from the sole trader who is using experience previously gained as a marketing manager to go freelance, to well-staffed and prestigious marketing and communication agencies.

Small and medium-sized companies tend to avoid taking on completely inexperienced recruits except at very junior levels. An agency with only a dozen staff will have limited resources to train new employees and will want everybody to pull their weight as quickly as possible. Consequently, many people move to an agency or consultancy after they have worked within the marketing function of a larger company and have a proven track record.

As we said before, there is considerable overlap between advertising, marketing and PR. A client who goes to a marketing consultant or agency may ask them to provide a full-service – to develop a marketing strategy, create advertisements and publicity materials, and to co-ordinate direct mail campaigns.

One marketing company that we spent time with offers the following services: strategic planning, market research, graphic design, direct marketing, advertising, public relations, media planning and buying, exhibition and event organisation, and the facility to design Internet and multi-media marketing. Staff range from account handlers and directors through to specialists such as designers, copywriters and a dedicated PR manager. Look back at the section in this book on jobs in advertising (page 12) to find out more about individual roles – although the focus of the work is different, the responsibilities are similar.

If you want to pursue a career in this field, then start your research now. Marketing strategy and tactics are fascinating and there is no shortage of books that will give you insights into how some of the blue-chip companies have planned campaigns to put their products at the front of the minds of customers.

Case Study
Marketing manager, retail chain

I worked for five years in fast moving consumer goods marketing, and then decided to extend my experience by moving into retail marketing. I'm now marketing manager for a chain of high street health and beauty retailers.

Our marketing function manages our brands and helps them to maintain their position in the market – we have to market products in a way that makes customers want to buy them. We work with other parts of the organisation, such as buying and retail management, to develop our strategies. We're also closely involved with customer focus groups and market research agencies to keep us in touch with our customers' perceptions.

I'm responsible for communications for my area of the company, and that includes all advertising and PR. It's a big challenge because we are trying to change the image of our stores and give them a more contemporary feel. I don't work on just one project or product – I'm trying to bring about major change in our whole marketing strategy.

I come into the office about 8am and sort through my mail and e-mails. There are a lot of meetings throughout the day, with members of my own team, executives further up the company and the external advertising and PR agencies who service our accounts. I'm working with them to develop marketing plans for the future and to monitor current campaigns. If I'm not in meetings, I try to spend as much time as possible in our stores, watching and listening. How else do I find out whether our strategies are working?

I have to prioritise, to plan how I will spend my time and stick to it. It's not always easy. There's too much to do in too short a time – it's just not possible to complete all the jobs yourself. That's why the team culture is so important in this type of work. I believe that you need a strong team to create a good marketing department. You have to trust the people you work with and have as much confidence in their abilities as you have in your own.

PUBLIC RELATIONS

'There are a million definitions of public relations. I have found it to be the craft of arranging the truth so that people will like you.'

Alan Harrington, American writer

More earnestly, the Institute of Public Relations defines PR as:

> '... the planned and sustained effort to establish and maintain goodwill and mutual understanding between an organisation and its publics.'

PR is about spreading a message through the media, face to face or through internal communications.

- A restaurant organises a launch party at its new premises – that is PR.
- A retail organisation sends out press releases to pre-empt bad news about its share price – that is PR.
- The Government organises press conferences and media interviews to publicise a fall in unemployment – that is PR.
- A small engineering company takes a group of its clients for a day at the races – that is PR.
- A utility company publishes a range of reports on everything from its finances to its commitment to community development – that is PR.
- A bank regularly sends every member of staff a magazine featuring news about the organisation, competitions and gossip – that is PR.

Unfairly, public relations sometimes has a rather lightweight image. In fact, it is a vital management function. The reputation and credibility of any organisation or individual will influence their success and achievements. It is the PR function that maintains this reputation and credibility.

Successful PR is about far more than hosting successful parties and arranging corporate hospitality at Wimbledon. It demands careful analysis and planning. PR can cost a lot of money, so consultants need to assure their clients that they can produce results. To launch and carry out an effective campaign demands extensive research and planning.

As a PR consultant, you need to identify and understand your audience and address a number of issues:

- Who do you want to build a relationship with?
- How does your audience think?

- What impresses them – or turns them away?
- What is the reason for your PR exercise? Are you aiming to create a new relationship, reinforce an existing one, or change the audience's perceptions of your client's products or services?

When you have answered those basic questions, you can start thinking about your PR strategy. How will you achieve your objectives? How long do you have to put your plan into action – and how much money is there in the budget? Do your ideas of good PR coincide with your client's? Or do they have a different concept of what makes a good approach? When your strategy is agreed with your client – and this may cover a PR programme that lasts several years – you can start organising.

Throughout the process, all your ideas and tactics will be firmly grounded on research and you will be continually monitoring results. Clients are not going to pay hundreds of thousands of pounds for you to organise PR events that raise your profile rather than their own!

The PR industry

There are an estimated 48,000 people working in public relations in the UK and, according to the Institute of Public Relations (IPR), the rate of growth in jobs in this area has been higher than for any other management function over the last 15 years.

PR companies vary in size and scope. There are plenty of 'one-man bands' around the country which handle public and media relations for local companies or which practise in a specialist field. Then there are the major players which handle PR for large organisations and turn over millions of pounds every year. These agencies will have the expertise to handle a wide range of tasks, many of which are linked with marketing and advertising.

A typical medium-sized PR company that we looked at advertises a range of services including:

- media management – editorials, promotions, reports, advertorials and specialist advertising. Effective media

management will give clients consistently good editorial coverage in the press, on radio and television
- events management – product launches, conferences, roadshows, presentations and media events
- sponsorship management – planning, negotiating and managing relationships between manufacturers or service providers and their sponsors
- internal communications – staff publications and events.

Another service that some PR companies offer is crisis management. If a management issue, such as a take-over bid, threatens the stability of an organisation, then the company will have to work on a number of fronts to allay the fears of its employees, customers and shareholders. Crisis management involves carrying out effective damage limitation, offering support and liaising between the various levels of the organisation, its customers, suppliers and associates. Most importantly, it includes working closely with the press to avoid hostile media coverage.

Many organisations build up very close relationships with their PR agencies and use them as sounding boards for any projected policy changes. A good PR consultant can offer valuable advice not only about managing a crisis, but also about how a crisis can be avoided in the first place.

As with marketing consultancies, some PR companies specialise in a particular business sector, such as financial PR, but many more will work in a diverse range of markets. Larger companies may offer an international PR facility either through branch offices or networking with locally based agencies in other countries. This service is particularly useful for clients who have a world market for their goods or services.

> 'Most of our clients are law firms. Over the years, we have built up a specialist team of PR executives who understand, and have good contacts within, the legal world. We handle many different tasks for clients, including producing publicity and marketing brochures, dealing with the press on their behalf and organising corporate events and hospitality.'
>
> *PR manager*

Kings of spin

In October 1999, Channel 4's programme *The Power List* rated Alistair Campbell as the sixth most powerful person in this country. His official title is Prime Minister's press secretary; his job involves writing the Prime Minister's press articles, organising ministers' media appearances and vetting their speeches.

His ranking among the great and the good (and not so good) is testimony to the influence of those who practise the art of media relations. What goes into a newspaper or appears on television can make or break an individual, an institution or an organisation. Press officers such as Campbell wield enormous power over the way the rest of us think.

Many high-profile organisations employ press officers. These are public relations staff whose role is to liaise with the media. They will not be involved in organising events or schmoozing clients, but will spend their time with representatives of the media. It is not an easy job. Journalists can be demanding and intrusive; you know they are always looking for your weaknesses. However, a good press officer will work *with* media representatives rather than against them, and will understand the importance of never alienating anybody whose words might appear in public.

The Government, local authorities and large corporations employ dedicated press officers. It's a challenging job – and not one for the faint-hearted. If you do get it wrong, everybody will witness your fall from grace.

'My job involves a mix of reactive and proactive work. As well as responding to media queries about Government issues, we are also raising awareness and explaining policy. That can be very worthwhile, particularly if you are helping people to understand their rights or publicising a measure that can help to improve health or save lives. Unlike agency staff, we offer a 24-hour service – you could get a call at midnight from somebody who wants information. There's a lot of satisfaction from knowing that you are in the middle of things, though. Many of the issues we deal with will make the headlines the following day.'

Government press officer

JOBS IN PR

If you work in a small to medium-sized PR consultancy, you will find yourself handling a range of tasks similar to the ones we described for account handlers in advertising and marketing agencies, so look back at those sections (page 13). You will probably have your own client list, attend meetings to help clients determine their PR programme, organise events and carry out account administration.

You may also be writing press releases and company literature, taking charge of production management and making the coffee.

Larger agencies may employ specialist staff to handle media relations and they could have in-house copywriters and designers.

PR opportunities also exist within big companies since some organisations prefer their own staff (often within the marketing department) to handle PR rather than buying in the services of an external consultancy. There are numerous career opportunities for in-house PR staff, for both graduate recruits and those who start as a general assistant and work their way up through the department. Naturally, such jobs are much sought after and you may work in a number of other departments before you move into PR. Unless you can offer specialist experience and a particularly useful contacts list, you are unlikely to walk straight into a job in PR for a blue-chip company.

'There's a big difference between in-house PR and working for a consultancy. Working in-house, I was very focused on one client – my employer. Now I have a number of clients who offer different goods and services and I have to be equally well informed about all of them. I'm continually on the move between one client and the next. I also manage my own budgets now – something that demands a whole new set of skills. The diversity of my work now is a real challenge but I can understand why agency work doesn't suit everybody.'

Account director, PR consultancy

MYTH BUSTER

A career in PR is just one long party

PR relies heavily on creating a positive image and one way to do that is to create a strong feelgood factor. Hence, the launch party when lots of people get together to drink free booze, eat free food and smile for the cameras in support of a new product, place or service in which they have no interest whatsoever. For the guests, life may well be one long party, but for the PR staff who have put the event together...?

'You may find that you spend a lot of time at social occasions, but you will always be working. Letting your hair down, over-indulging and making an exhibition of yourself are not options. You have to remain alert, work the room, make sure that your guests are enjoying themselves and never lose sight of the fact that you are promoting something. That can still be great fun, but doing it night after night demands a lot of stamina, and a genuine willingness to talk to people you don't know — and probably don't want to know.'

Events co-ordinator, PR consultancy

A career in PR can be very exciting, take you to interesting places and put you in contact with some fascinating people. At the same time, it is very demanding. Sometimes you will be working with products/services/people that you genuinely believe in. Often you will be waxing lyrical about things that you find distinctly unappealing, old hat or just plain boring. You must apply the same degree of enthusiasm and dedication to putting across the message, regardless of your personal opinions.

'From the outside, PR looks like a very glamorous career – and in many ways it is. I regularly go to major sporting and cultural events with clients and I'm out at least three nights a week at parties, receptions or openings. I'd be lying if I said it wasn't fun. But it's also very tiring. Even if I've been at a client's party until nearly midnight, I still have to get up at 6am to get into the office. I still have the paperwork to handle and the meetings to attend. And I'm very conscious that I have to look alert and presentable all the time. It's fine at the moment because I'm young and enthusiastic, but I'm not sure how long I will want to go on coping with a lifestyle that intrudes so much on my personal space and free time.'

PR consultant

WOMEN IN ADVERTISING, MARKETING AND PR

The gender split in the advertising world is about 50/50, so this would appear to be an industry in which women have a fair chance of developing high-profile careers. Unfortunately, recent research suggests that, although women may be well represented numerically, they rarely make their presence felt at the very top of the industry. When *Media Guardian* surveyed the top 20 UK agencies in late 1999, it found that:

- none had a female chairperson
- only two had female chief executives – and one of these shared her position with a man
- there were no female managing directors or creative directors
- the number of all-female creative teams is negligible.

Women do tend to make their presence felt in support roles such as planning and account management, where many reach director level. But 'a genuine dearth of female talent right at the top of the industry and within the engine-room of advertising, the creative department, is alarming'.[4] What is even more alarming is that the situation has not shown any noticeable improvement since the Institute of Practitioners in Advertising (IPA) carried out extensive research into women in advertising ten years ago.

[4] *The Guardian*, 13 September 1999

Eighty per cent of advertising is targeted at women – yet the IPA census of employees states that only 6% of copywriters and 15% of creative directors are female.

Similar problems appear in marketing and PR, where women take their fair share (or more) of roles at junior or middle management levels, but are under-represented at the top.

There are a number of reasons for this. Female presence at senior board level is minimal in almost all industries; the glass ceiling appears to be still firmly in place in the UK employment market as a whole.

The demands of a career in advertising and marketing may also challenge women who want to have a family. The job is not nine-to-five and may require your presence at any time of the day or night. As well as the work you do in the office, you may also have to travel, socialise with clients and maintain extensive networks of contacts – all difficult if you have young children. Taking a career break is an option, but in an industry which moves so quickly (and is so full of new recruits hungry for your job) there is a chance that you won't be able to get back in.

'Like many agencies, ours is a small company and we don't have a lot of staff to absorb a prolonged absence from work. When I was pregnant, my boss and I agreed that I would work mainly from home for a few months after the birth. In principle that was fine, but I soon began to feel pressure to spend more time in the office. Nothing was ever said outright but it was implied that my absence created a lot of work for other people. It's a familiar story in a lot of companies that have a small core of staff.'

Account manager, communications agency

VITAL STATISTICS

We have looked at a selection of jobs in advertising, marketing and PR. Now read on to learn the 'vital statistics' of these industries and to find out what salaries and benefits packages you can anticipate.

This information is current at the time of writing (autumn 1999) and it gives a general idea of what is on offer. Because there are so many small and medium-sized companies operating in these industries, it is difficult to be precise about salary levels. What you earn will be largely dependent on your experience and capabilities, what your company can afford and your ability to drive a hard bargain.

Salaries

> 'Every month, we have approaches from young college graduates who offer to work for free for a few months just so they can get some experience. There is no shortage of people who want to work in this industry and, at the lower levels, they come cheap.'
>
> *Director, communications agency*

Are careers in advertising, marketing and PR well paid? No. If you are just starting your career as a college leaver or graduate, you will not be earning megabucks and you can expect a salary that is significantly lower than you might find in other industries.

However, as we have already said, careers can move quickly in the communications sector and it is not unusual for staff to rise to director level before they reach the age of 30. At that point, salaries can soar. Agencies will pay well to keep the staff they want, so you can anticipate attractive packages that include performance-related bonuses, company car, pension and private health cover. For the really gifted account executive or creative director, the rewards can be very high.

If you go to work in the marketing function of a major national or multinational company, then your salary will be more structured and will increase rather more slowly and steadily. Your starting salary will depend on the industry and the company for which you work. In many large companies, marketing trainees will start on the same scale as graduate trainees in any other department. Again, higher up the career scale, salaries are competitive and often accompanied by valuable benefits packages.

> 'Working in PR, I find that the packages are in line with other marketing disciplines. If you show flair and enthusiasm, you will be rewarded. Holidays may have to be cancelled but the perks are obvious – you get entrance to events that you would never normally attend and quite a lot of free samples, which is good if you are working on a product you can use!'
>
> *Account director, PR agency*

The following salary ranges indicate the levels of pay being offered for a range of jobs in London and the Home Counties at the end of 1999. Salaries vary enormously and youcan expect significantly lower packages if you work in the regions.

Advertising

- General assistant – college leaver with A levels or GNVQs: £9,000–£12,000.
- Graduate trainee: £14,000–£15,000.
- Account manager with three or four years' experience: £20,000–£25,000.
- Director: £40,000 plus bonuses. This can easily move into six figures for the real high flyers.

Marketing

- Marketing assistant – graduate with one or two years' experience: £12,000–£15,000.
- Graduate trainee: £16,000–£22,000 depending on the organisation you join.
- Marketing manager – graduate already working in a management role with two to five years' experience: £20,000–£30,000.
- Marketing director with a major manufacturing or retail organisation: £40,000 plus.

PR

- Starting salaries can be very low – again a reflection of the competition for jobs from people anxious to start a career in advertising, marketing or PR. Take this (regional) vacancy for a graduate trainee PR co-ordinator:

Main duties and responsibilities:
To run a new in-house PR department, generate media interest to both trade and consumer beauty press. Write press releases, meet and form relationships with beauty journalists, run the PR database and co-ordinate coverage on national, regional and local levels.

Experience and qualifications:
The suitable applicant will be educated to HE level with a degree in PR, Marketing or Communications with good computer skills. Good interpersonal skills both on a face-to-face basis and over the telephone. In-house training will be provided for those looking for a future in PR.

And for all that responsibility, you will earn the princely sum of £9,000 per annum.

Junior management attracts salaries around the £18,000–£25,000 mark. Further up the ladder, salaries improve and, as with advertising and marketing, if you make it to director level you can expect a high salary and impressive benefits package. Here is an ad for a PR account director:

An agency specialising in trade communications is looking for a PR Account Director with an in-depth knowledge of the drinks and fmcg markets and strong strategic skills to develop business-to-business communications programmes for blue-chip clients.
The successful candidate must have the ability to think 'outside the box' and generate opportunities and angles for trade press coverage beyond the usual brand news stories and product features. Excellent client liaison skills essential for networking across sales and marketing functions and at board director level. Package circa £35K.

Working conditions

These are usually good, and often exceptional. Advertising, marketing and PR companies are in the business of promoting an image so they usually start with their own. Most companies will invest in their premises to give their clients the right impression, so expect clean, vibrant surroundings. Of course, there are exceptions and you may come across a successful agency that consists of dark, cluttered and airless rooms. But the majority of agencies and consultancies we visited offered superb working environments.

Some companies are experimenting with new ways of working, such as hot desking, where staff have no personal workstation but wander around the premises clutching their mobile phones and laptop computers. This, it has been argued, breaks down boundaries and stimulates creativity. Then there is the advertising agency with the games room and the sauna...

In principle, all three industries work standard office hours, but in practice staff are expected to put in a lot more. If you have to meet a deadline or make a presentation then leaving on the dot of 5.30pm is not an option. Flexibility and a willingness to work long hours and weekends are prerequisites. If you are not willing to do that, the company will soon find somebody who will.

'I get into the office at about 8.30am and rarely leave before 7.30pm. If we have a rush job on, then I'll come in at weekends and I regularly take work home. It's not a problem because I like what I'm doing but it can be hard on family and friends. There have been plenty of times when I've cancelled a social engagement because something's come up at work. You have to be willing to do that – this isn't a nine-to-five job.'

Creative director, marketing consultancy

'I generally work from about 7.30am to 7pm or 8pm. I also travel a lot so may have to set off at the crack of dawn to get to a meeting or a launch and then not get home until midnight.'

Account director, PR agency

Always check out the benefits package. What you are offered will depend on your level of employment and how desirable your talents are – companies will put themselves out to retain the right staff. Many will offer a pension and private health cover to all employees. Other sweeteners that we have come across include company cars or subsidised transport, free health club membership, use of a holiday home in Ireland, regular 'team building' nights out at the best restaurants in town... the list is long.

One final word of caution. Make sure that you are absolutely clear about the terms and conditions of employment before you accept a job. Many agencies and consultancies are small and fairly informal in structure so they can be rather slow in presenting you with a written contract. You need to know:

- when and how salary is reviewed
- who is involved in the review process
- whether you will take part in an appraisal scheme
- opportunities for promotion
- how much notice is required by either you or the company to terminate employment.

It makes life far easier in the long run if you know exactly where you stand.

> 'Early in my career I worked for a small PR company. At the interview, I was told that my starting salary would be reviewed after six months and that all staff got a Christmas bonus. Six months after I started, nothing happened and I didn't feel comfortable raising the subject with the managing director. No bonus was mentioned in December, either. Finally, I talked to one of my colleagues about it and she just laughed. Evidently we were all promised the same but bonuses and pay reviews only happened when the boss felt like it! Of course, I could have made a fuss but I had nothing in writing and it was a small company – I would have been very uncomfortable making waves. I wasn't so trusting the next time I applied for a job and asked for a written statement of the terms and conditions.'
>
> *PR manager*

This section on the vital statistics brings you to the end of the first part of *The Insider Career Guide to Advertising, Marketing and PR*. So far, you've considered the background to, and some different types of, jobs in these industries. In Part Two, we look at the person and focus on the skills and personal qualities that help recruits to the industry succeed.

part two the person

the person

Introduction

Part One of *The Insider Career Guide to Advertising, Marketing and PR* looked at what these industries involve, their culture and some of the jobs that might be available to you.

In this section, we look at the skills and personal qualities that could help you get ahead in advertising, marketing and PR. What are employers looking for when they recruit new staff? What makes one candidate stand out from the rest?

First, however, you need to take a look at yourself. A lot of people, misled by the image of high excitement and good times, believe that they want a career in advertising, marketing or PR. What they don't do is take a critical look at themselves to see if they have the right sort of personality for this type of work.

KNOW YOURSELF

Too many of us think, 'I want to be... (insert your own choice of words here)' without examining whether we are psychologically suited for the type of work we select. Consequently, we get the person who goes into sales but does not have the force of character to close a deal. We come across writers who cannot cope with the isolation that their work demands. We find people who are naturally reticent struggling to deal with the public, and individualists who end up in highly structured organisations where they must toe the company line. If we analysed ourselves more *before* we started applying for jobs, fewer of us might be unhappy once we got them.

Carrying out a personal analysis to determine what sort of career is appropriate for you is a complicated business.

In a book of this length, we cannot do more than offer you a few guidelines.

If you are unsure about your career choice and whether it 'fits' your personality, then think about taking professional advice.

- **Talk to careers advisers** at your college or university if you are still in full-time education. Alternatively, talk to the staff at your local JobCentre and find out what careers guidance services are available in your area.
- **Find a private careers guidance organisation.** Some of these will offer a comprehensive service to audit your skills, attitudes and experience to highlight areas in which you might excel. They can also help you to locate vacancies, prepare your CV, coach you for interviews and advise you on whether to accept a job. Choose a reputable organisation and ask what they charge before you sign up – some of them can be very expensive. Careers guidance specialists advertise in careers literature, newspaper careers supplements, the *Yellow Pages* and on the Internet.
- **Look at literature** in your local library and bookstores. There are plenty of books to help you carry out a self-audit, although this method will not guarantee you impartial advice!

WHAT DO YOU WANT?

If your only reason for considering a job in advertising, marketing or PR is to earn money, then you should start looking at other careers. The competition is too great (and the salaries at junior levels are too low) for these industries to appeal to anyone whose attitude to work is 'just a job that pays the bills'.

Similarly, if you think that these areas offer the chance for working life to become one long party, then think again. Yes, you may find aspects of your life lively and interesting and you may work with very sociable people. You may also be paid to go to parties. But don't be fooled; above all you will be expected to work hard. Look back at the first section of this book and you will see that a common feature in our interviews was the emphasis people put on the amount of work and pressure they had to cope with.

So why do you want to become an account executive, a graphic designer or a PR consultant? What do you expect these careers to offer you? It's worth making a brief list of your expectations now, before you start applying for jobs. Alternatively, try our quiz. It will help you to find out more about yourself and what you really want from your career. This is not a psychometric test but it will give you some insights into your personality and your suitability for a career in the communications industry.

About you...

Answer yes or no to the following questions.

	Yes	No
1. Will you be happy working in an office?	☐	☐
2. Are you ambitious?	☐	☐
3. Are you fairly shy?	☐	☐
4. Do you have good communication skills?	☐	☐
5. Are you interested in modern culture?	☐	☐
6. Is job security important to you?	☐	☐
7. Are you willing to move frequently from one job to the next?	☐	☐
8. Is earning a lot of money important to you?	☐	☐
9. Are you keen to get your opinions across to others?	☐	☐
10. Do you have high standards of literacy and numeracy?	☐	☐
11. Do you like working in teams?	☐	☐
12. Do you like working with people?	☐	☐
13. Does criticism upset you?	☐	☐
14. Are you looking for a formalised career structure?	☐	☐

If you answered yes to questions 1, 2, 4, 5, 7, 9, 10, 11 and 12, you are showing many of the attitudes essential for work in advertising, marketing and PR. If you answered yes to questions 3, 6, 8, 13 and 14 then these may not be the industries for you. Are you sure you have the commitment and nerve to fight your way to the top?

Now answer these questions.

1. During a job interview, you are asked to sing a song. Do you:

   a. take a deep breath and launch into a rousing chorus of, 'I'll tell you what I want, what I really, really want…'
   b. refuse. This is a job interview, not an audition for the chorus line
   c. ask what the interviewer wants you to sing
   d. leave?

2. You have to give a presentation to a client. Do you:

   a. wait until the last minute to prepare because you're so busy
   b. spend a lot of time preparing before the day
   c. think that preparation is for wimps
   d. go sick and let somebody else do it?

3. Do you think teamwork is:

   a. a chance for other people to steal your glory
   b. a waste of time – few people really work well in teams
   c. a necessary evil – it must be seen to be done
   d. essential in a busy workplace?

4. You walk into a party where you don't know any of the other guests. Do you:

   a. seek out another Billy No-mates and stand next to them
   b. look for the liveliest group of people in the room and introduce yourself
   c. stare out of the window
   d. refuse all invitations to parties except those held by your closest friends?

5. Your boss asks you to think 'outside the box'. Do you

   a. go and work in the garden
   b. look for a new angle on a problem
   c. ask which software program you should be using
   d. berate him/her for using unintelligible jargon?

6. A client tells you your marketing ideas are unsuitable. Do you:

   a. tell them that they are wrong – you're the expert
   b. burst into tears
   c. ask them to explain what they don't like about your suggestions
   d. switch off while they talk – clients can be such a pain?

7. Your boss asks you to work through the night to complete a piece of work. Do you:

   a. refuse? On your salary there's no way you'll stay after 5.30pm
   b. agree and get on with it
   c. ask how much it's worth for you to stay
   d. agree but make sure that everybody knows how much you are put upon?

8. You think people who care about their appearance are:

   a. sad. Haven't they anything better to do?
   b. shallow. No amount of money will detract from their personality defects
   c. sensible. What you see reflects what you get
   d. lucky. You have no time to make yourself look smart.

9. When you are out with a group of people do you:

   a. find it hard to get your viewpoint across because nobody listens to you
   b. tend to dominate the conversation
   c. try to make sure that everybody gets an equal chance to share their opinions
   d. clam up. You hate social occasions?

ich of the following would you find it easy to be usiastic about:

ngine oil

b. a new car design

c. tampons

d. fish fingers.

Give yourself the following points:

1a. 3	1b. 1	1c. 2	1d. 0
2a.2	2b. 3	2c.1	2d. 0
3a. 1	3b. 0	3c. 2	3d. 3
4a. 2	4b. 3	4c. 1	4d. 0
5a. 0	5b. 3	5c. 1	5d. 2
6a. 2	6b. 0	6c. 3	6d. 1
7a. 0	7b. 3	7c. 2	7d. 1
8a. 1	8b. 0	8c. 3	8d. 2
9a. 1	9b. 2	9c. 3	9d. 0
10a. 3	10b. 3	10c. 3	10d. 3

The higher your score the better! If you have 30–39 points, then you definitely have the attitudes and bare-faced nerve that will help you to stand out from the crowd when you apply for jobs. 24–30 points suggest that you stand a good chance of succeeding in these industries. Less than 24 and you may need to think again – is this really what you want to do with your life?

WHAT DO EMPLOYERS WANT?

Once you have examined your own aptitudes and desires, it is time to think about what employers want. No business can afford to take people on just because they like the look of them. Employees need certain skills and personal qualities that will make them good at their job. So, what are advertising, marketing and PR companies looking for?

In many smaller advertising, marketing and PR agencies staff multi-task. Employers will be looking for good all-rounders with highly developed communication skills. In larger agencies, the skills base for an account manager will be different to that of a creative or planner – although some factors such as teamworking and presentation skills will be required for all functions.

Here we look at some of the skills that employers frequently ask for. Because there is considerable overlap between advertising, marketing and PR (and the same recruitment phrases tend to come up for all three) we have focused on skills areas, rather than looking at particular jobs in each industry.

The qualities we examine are taken from 'person specifications' for a variety of jobs and from interviews with people who recruit staff. This recruitment advertisement for an account manager is fairly typical in the skills and aptitudes it demands.

We need a born communicator, a motivated and quality-driven individual, a dynamic and persuasive personality who is capable of selling ideas both internally and externally to clients. You will have the ability to oversee, motivate and support designers. You should be an excellent team player who enjoys being responsible for your own work, and you should be happy working to deadlines. Your work should be highly creative in meeting the brief, sympathetic to the brand and be produced within budget.

Communication skills

It would seem to be very obvious that somebody working in a communication-based industry will need well-honed communication skills. What many people don't understand is what those communication skills involve and what they will be used for.

'It's surprising how few people communicate effectively. They can talk for England but they simply cannot listen, and they can't interpret what is being said to them. As an account handler, I'm bringing together the needs of my client with the capabilities of the team in my agency. Clients are not always sure what they want so I have to be able to listen to them and to some extent read their minds. Listening is the hardest part – it's very easy during a meeting or a pitch to get carried away by your own ideas and to dominate a conversation. You may give a great performance but ultimately you're not going to understand your client and their aims.'

Account manager, marketing company

The term 'communication skills' covers a number of different areas, including:

- speaking clearly, fluently and convincingly
- listening
- understanding and responding to non-verbal communication (body language)
- producing effective written communications, including briefs and presentations.

If you work in account management, you will deal with many different people both inside and outside your agency. You may be talking to the managing director of a major organisation in the morning, briefing your creative team at lunchtime and researching with focus groups from all socio-economic backgrounds in the afternoon. You will need to be absolutely clear what you want from each person and this may involve communicating at a variety of different levels using different 'languages' with each audience. 'USP' may be a term in daily use within your office, but it won't make a lot of sense to a test audience of 16 year-olds. (See *Jargon buster* on page 89.)

> 'I think briefing the creative team is an art in itself. You have to take back the client's message and make sure the copywriters and art director know exactly what is required. Our creative team rarely meets the clients so I'm the intermediary and the only source of information. If my brief isn't clear, there's a risk that the team will produce something that the client won't like. The guys I work with are great because they are happy to work to a tight brief and take guidance. But in the past I've worked with some real prima donnas who felt that their creative instincts should be given full rein, regardless of what the client wanted or what budgets were available. They needed very careful handling!'
>
> *Account manager, marketing company*

Highly developed communication skills will be the first thing any employer looks for, whatever role you are applying for. You should also be highly literate, with a good command of grammar and spelling, and a genuine feel for language. Whether you are writing materials or producing briefs and presentations, you cannot afford to make mistakes.

Teamworking skills

'A good team player' is a description to which many people aspire but few genuinely attain. Most of us are competitive by nature and working for group, rather than individual, recognition is not easy. However, small or medium-sized companies thrive on teamwork and the ability to pull together with colleagues is one quality you will be expected to demonstrate.

Account managers will work as part of a team and may have to direct it at the same time. You must be receptive to other people's ideas but, at the same time, you must ensure that colleagues deliver what is required of them. You may have to exert a high degree of control to ensure that your team meets tight deadlines and budgetary restraints. You will need to motivate your team, particularly when the initial concept stages are complete and the generation of exciting ideas gives way to the hard slog of completing a job.

> 'Good PR professionals like working in teams to foster good practice. You have to be willing to take on board another person's point of view. Your team members need to be committed to getting results and to helping each other.'
>
> *Account director, PR agency*

Most of the companies we talked to stressed the importance of a strong team culture in every function of the business. It helps them to produce results by maximising staff resources and sharing knowledge. If you are uneasy working closely with other people, you may want to reconsider whether advertising, marketing and PR are the right industries for you.

Organisational skills

As we have already suggested, if you work in a small agency or consultancy, you may be responsible for many different functions, including client liaison, research, co-ordinating the creative process and overseeing production. You will be meeting people, planning schedules and keeping everyone informed. And, as you may be working on a number of different accounts at once, you will be switching from one task to another and from one client to another throughout the day.

To do all this without panicking, getting stressed out or losing the plot, demands good organisational skills. You need to be able to prioritise jobs, keep a diary, produce and monitor progress charts.

The same organisational skills are needed in the marketing function of any large organisation. You will find that other departments make demands on your time and that you spend a lot of your time in meetings. Again, the abilities to prioritise and carry out your work systematically are very important.

'I spend the first hour of every morning just checking correspondence and sorting out my schedule for the rest of the day. E-mail has drastically increased my workload – I may have a couple of dozen messages waiting when I log on, all of which have to be sifted through and dealt with. During the day I'll have meetings scheduled with other people in the company, such as accountants or my own line manager. Then there are suppliers to deal with – the agencies, printers, video producers. At the same time, I've work to be getting on with to prepare new marketing strategies. The hardest part is deciding what to do first.'

Marketing manager, retail chain

In PR, it takes a lot of organisational skill to make an event run smoothly. You could be co-ordinating the activities of dozens of people, organising caterers, transport, flowers, invitations, venues, printers and making sure that they all deliver what you want, when you want it. You have to keep tight control and learn not to panic when things go wrong.

Analytical skills

A good advertising, marketing or PR campaign will be the result of careful targeting and painstaking research as well as creative and innovative brilliance. Whatever capacity you work in, you should be able to evaluate data, draw valid conclusions from it and apply those conclusions in your work.

In advertising and marketing, there are some interesting opportunities in research and planning, even though these jobs may not have the initial 'glamour appeal' of account management, art direction or copywriting.

Researchers should understand the principles and applications of quantitative and qualitative research. Larger agencies (or specialist research and media planning companies) will be interested in recruits who have relevant qualifications, such as a degree in an analytical discipline such as mathematics, statistics, psychology or economics. If this is your chosen field of employment, then you need to be literate as well as numerate so you can prepare reports and presentations for both clients and members of your own team.

Media planners also need to have an understanding of demographics and socio-economics to help them understand how target audiences work. At the same time there is a creative element to a planner's work, since they will be responsible for determining what media will provide the best results for the client.

Financial awareness

In an ideal world, creating the right advertisement, marketing campaign or PR launch would be the aim, and money would be no object. Unfortunately, this is the real world where budgets and profit margins shape our actions. It doesn't matter how good your ideas are; they will not be used if they are too expensive.

The ability to stick to a budget is important for everybody in an agency or consultancy, particularly for those working in account management, media buying or creative services. You will find that a lot of your time is taken up in negotiating with your clients and your suppliers. You want as much money as you can get from the former and the lowest charges from the latter. Good negotiating skills and financial acumen will raise your value to your employer.

Personal qualities

The same words appear again and again in recruitment advertisements for jobs in advertising, marketing and PR: *confident, extrovert, dynamic, able to work under pressure, motivated, enthusiastic...*

Stamina and enthusiasm are very important, since jobs in these industries can make heavy demands on both your time and energy. Most agency staff we talked to do not work regular hours and are accustomed to burning the midnight oil to meet tight deadlines. To withstand these demands you need to love what you do, rather than seeing it as 'just a job'.

Flexibility is also important, plus a willingness to turn your hand to any task, particularly when you are starting out on your career. There are mundane and tedious elements in every job and you have to accept these as gracefully as the more challenging and high-profile work. Just because your job specification has you listed as an account manager does not mean that you won't find yourself stuffing envelopes with press releases, manning the telephones, taking minutes in a meeting or spending hours analysing research data.

The ability to adapt to a variety of tasks will stand you in good stead, particularly if you work in small or medium-sized agencies where limits on the numbers of core staff mean that everyone has to pull together to keep the business going.

Tact and diplomacy are invaluable. As we said in the section on communication skills, you will spend your days talking to a lot of different people. They may not always have the same ideas as you, they may not agree with you, you may not particularly like them. Nevertheless, you have to work with them, influence them and motivate them. That demands sensitivity in your dealings with other people, an ability to empathise and a genuine willingness to respect their opinions and feelings.

'It's hard not to get a bit arrogant when you work with a lot of talented, extrovert people. You tend to think that everyone is – or should be – like you. And we tend to move in fairly small social and professional circles so may not get enough exposure to the world outside. However, that arrogance can cost you a lot if you don't keep it under control. We once tested some artwork with a focus group. They didn't like it but the marketing manager thought it was brilliant because it was so different to anything he'd seen before. His actual comment was, 'What do they know? – they're only members of the public.' He ran the materials and they attracted a lot of criticism. He'd forgotten the basic rule that it is members of the public that make any campaign a success.'

Account director, marketing agency

'What personal characteristics help in this type of work? Patience, diplomacy, excellent time-management skills, creativity and the ability to work well under pressure. You also have to be able to cope with the negative aspects of the job – it can be demotivating when you have difficult clients who won't buy into your ideas.'

Account director, PR agency

QUALIFICATIONS

Advertising, marketing and PR are industries where academic and professional qualifications are less important than talent, experience – and either good contacts or a lot of luck to get your first break. Recruits come from many different educational backgrounds, although increasingly they will be graduates who can show an ability to assimilate and process information rapidly and accurately. What you will need to break into these careers are:

- excellent literacy and numeracy skills
- some knowledge of business procedures
- computer literacy. At the very least you will probably be doing all your own clerical work, letters and proposals. At best, you will have a good working knowledge of CD-ROM, the Internet and interactive TV development, all of which are becoming increasingly important as advertising takes more and more advantage of new media opportunities.

For more information about qualifications and entry into each of the industries, look at Part Three of this book.

CREATIVES

Because so many people are attracted to the idea of working in copywriting and design, we are giving creatives a separate section of their own.

Good creatives will have many of the qualities we identified previously, such as highly developed communication and teamworking skills, enthusiasm and dedication – all of these are essential if you are going to make your mark. Business awareness also helps so that you appreciate the importance of deadlines and budgets.

> 'You say to people "I'm a copywriter" and they have this totally unreal idea of what you do. They think you sit around, the words just flash into your head, you write them down and then you spend the rest of the week out to lunch. Of course, it's nothing like that. You work long hours, you have to be very disciplined and you have to cope with the pressure to produce original and innovative work all the time. You're only as good as your last job so you can't afford to have too many off-days.'
>
> *Copywriter, marketing agency*

Copywriters come from all sorts of backgrounds. This is definitely an area where qualifications are secondary to that elusive quality – talent. A good copywriter is articulate and can communicate effectively, clearly and economically. They have a feel for language that allows them to put words together in a way that stimulates an emotional or intellectual response in their audience. They also have the skill to refine and polish their words to get the effect they want. It may sound easy. It's not.

On a more practical level, all writers need a first-class command of the English language, including the technical aspects of grammar and spelling; they need to understand when to use 'fewer' rather than 'less', when to use a subjunctive and the difference in meaning between 'practise' and 'practice'. And, if the websites of some major advertising companies are anything to go by, these skills are currently in short supply!

Some copywriters specialise in a certain type of writing, such as producing corporate handbooks, technical documents, user manuals or script writing. You can have a lucrative career if you find your niche, since specialist skills are always in demand. Alternatively, some writers will work in a particular industry, such as computers or engineering, where their specialist knowledge can be put to good effect.

'My background is in preparing training materials. It's a fairly specialised area and you can make a good living if you have the right contacts, experience and market yourself successfully. But I've worked in a lot of other areas as well – corporate publicity, technical manuals, direct marketing materials. You use a different style of writing for each one so maybe that's my real specialism – the ability to turn out words that suit a particular audience.'

Freelance copywriter

Creative directors, graphic designers and website designers need a proven talent for drawing or design. Computers may have taken away much of the hard graft in the creative process, but you still need the visual expertise to put shapes and colours together. Most people who work in this field have some formal qualifications in either commercial art or a graphic arts discipline.

Larger agencies may have staff specialising in finished arts, whose job is to work up the original ideas and concepts into finished artwork. This is skilled work and demands training and experience as well as a thorough understanding of the computer applications now used in design, as this job advertisement shows.

Talented Versatile Interactive Designers – must have a strong background in interface design and animation for Web, CD-ROM and DVD (or other TV-viewed format). Skills must include Photoshop, Flash, Dreamweaver, Fireworks and Java Script. Ideally you will be familiar with animation tools such as After Effects.

Plenty of people complete the right courses, but only a few will move on to develop really successful careers as art directors.

'The quality of applicants for jobs is not good. I'd say that 98% of graphic designers are not creative – they merely copy other people's ideas. They bring me portfolios with the latest styles and design trends. They show that they can follow fashion, but I want more than that. It's no good using a particular style because it's trendy if it has no relevance to the target audience. We look for original thought within a commercial framework – people who are really aware of the client's needs, can communicate effectively and can work within the constraints of a business.'

Managing director, marketing and communications agency

AND FINALLY...

Make no mistake, the competition for jobs in advertising, marketing and PR is fierce and you will be up against a lot of highly talented, intelligent and skilled people. One quality that can make you succeed where others fail is passion. You have to want to work in your chosen field, to feel strongly about this type of work and to have the persistence to convince employers that you are worth considering for a vacancy.

'What am I looking for when I recruit new staff? I want somebody who is passionate about advertising and who can talk with real knowledge and enthusiasm about ads. You get a lot of approaches from people who think they might want to try a career in advertising because it sounds interesting and glamorous. They don't get very far, either in this agency or anywhere else. There are so many good people out there that we can afford to hold out for the very best and to me that is the candidate who is totally involved in the industry.'

Associate partner, advertising agency

'We expect applicants to have qualifications and experience that are relevant to us – I don't really want to query them on that. What I want to know is what extra they can offer. Can they go beyond the obvious, because that's what they'll have to do to give our clients the best value. I can usually recognise the sort of person we want within a few seconds: 98% of the people we see are average and that's not good enough. We're looking for people who are inquisitive, who want to know more for their clients. In fact, we're shocked when people don't overperform. This industry is about overperformance.'

Managing director, marketing and communications agency

In Part Two of *The Insider Career Guide to Advertising, Marketing and PR*, you have looked at some of the skills and personal qualities that you need if you want to make progress in these industries.

Part Three, *Getting in, Getting on... Getting out*, considers in some detail:

- getting into the industry – how to apply for jobs and what to expect as you go through the application process
- getting on – opportunities for advancing your career
- getting out – what careers you could look at next if you decide to move out of advertising, marketing or PR.

part three

getting in, getting on... getting out

getting in, getting on... getting out

Introduction

The third part of *The Insider Career Guide to Advertising, Marketing and PR* focuses on how you can get into these industries, how you can get on and climb the career ladder and how, if you want, you can eventually move into other areas of employment.

As we keep saying, competition to get into these industries is fierce. How can you make your application stand out from the rest so that you get past the initial stages of selection and into an interview? What strategies have other job applicants used to get their feet into the doors of advertising and PR agencies and consultancies, and into the marketing departments of large organisations?

If you are invited to interview, how should you present yourself? What are selectors looking for? And what can put them off? Once you've found the opportunity you were looking for, how will your career take shape? Can you speed up your progress through training and professional qualifications?

Finally, if you've spent a few years in advertising, marketing and PR and you want to get out (yes, some people do decide they've had enough!), where can you use your skills and experience next?

By talking to both interviewees who have successfully won the jobs they wanted, and to recruiters and selectors in these industries, we've put together some simple but valuable advice to help you through all stages of the application and advancement process. Read on to find out more about applications and CVs, interviews, training, qualifications and the route to success.

GETTING IN

You won't have any problems finding advertising, marketing and PR agencies anywhere in the country but, unless you are in London or one of the regional capitals such as Manchester or Birmingham, they may well be small companies with a fairly localised client base. There are some exceptions, but after talking to professionals within the industry the consensus was clear: London is still the centre and the place where the big names base themselves.

> 'There is still a north–south divide and London is still the hub. However much the industry is trying to correct this, it's changing extremely slowly. Where you choose to work can have a big impact on your career. Some people are better suited to small agencies, others want to work within a large organisation — and to do that you'll probably end up down south.'
>
> *New business director, marketing*

If you want to work within the marketing section of a large organisation, then you will obviously be based where the company sends you. You could end up in London – or Luton or Loughborough.

THE JOB MARKET

Before we look at ways in which you can make your applications stand out from the rest, it is useful to look at the recruitment process through the eyes of the recruiters themselves. Yes, there is probably a higher ratio of applicants per vacancy in advertising, marketing and PR than many other employment areas, but recruiters still face the same problems of finding the right person to fill their vacancy.

In 1999, the Institute of Personnel and Development (IPD) published a report on recruitment[1] which revealed that nearly three-quarters of all employers (regardless of industry) were experiencing difficulties in recruiting staff. The biggest problem they faced was a lack of required or relevant experience, closely followed by a lack of technical skills.

Advertising, marketing and PR companies face the same problems. There may be hundreds of applicants for a single

[1] *IPD Survey Report 5 – Recruitment*, Institute of Personnel and Development, August 1999

vacancy, many of whom have the right attitude, masses of enthusiasm and are just looking for the opportunity to learn the business. The problem is that if you run a small, busy agency or consultancy with a limited number of core staff, you will not have the resources to train up inexperienced or unskilled recruits. You need somebody who can walk into the office on Monday morning and start pulling their weight by lunchtime – at the latest.

What can you, in your search for a job, learn from that information? First, that experience counts.

WORK EXPERIENCE

It is easy to say that experience counts, but if you are fresh out of school or college the chances are your experience will be very limited. How can you get into the industry, learn more about it and, most importantly, gain that valuable experience that will add value to your CV?

Start early. If you are studying, look for any placements or vacation work that will get you inside a company, even if it is only for a couple of weeks. Be prepared to work for nothing (or a pittance) and to do the most menial of jobs. It doesn't matter if you spend two weeks licking stamps and making the tea – you will still learn a lot about the culture, language and practices of the industry.

To get placements or work experience, check out the following.

- **Your college placement service.** If your course of study involves placements, they should be able to help you find periods of work with appropriate companies. In the first instance, be clear about the sort of work experience you are looking for and ask specifically for advertising, marketing or PR. If there are no appropriate vacancies, you can broaden your search later.
- **Local agencies and consultancies.** You may have to cold call them by sending a polite letter asking if they can take you on for a couple of weeks. Give precise times when you are available for work. Make

it clear that you are studying and want to enter the industry when you qualify. Accept that this scattergun approach can involve sending out dozens of letters and accept rejections gracefully. If you are persistent enough, somebody will take you on.

- **Employment agencies.** If you have relevant skills (such as word processing, reception skills, etc.) you may be able to get temporary work. All right, you won't be going in to join the creative team on your first day, but it will give you contacts and an insight into the industry.
- **JobCentres.** Again, you are not likely to find an ad for an art director down at the local JobCentre, but you might find a vacancy for a college leaver trainee or for a clerical assistant or administrator.
- **Personal contacts.** Advertising, marketing and PR are industries where word-of-mouth referrals are particularly important. Employment is fluid, people change jobs frequently, so within agencies the recruitment process is often bypassed. Who do you know who works in the industry? Do your parents have contacts – do your friends' parents have contacts? Do you know anybody who works for a large organisation that has a marketing department? Can they put in a word for you? Tell as many people as possible that you are looking for some practical experience in your chosen field and beg for help.
- **Charities and voluntary organisations.** Many of these organisations will take on unpaid staff to help with promotions. Some of the larger charities offer work experience schemes in PR and fund-raising. Your local branch of a smaller charity may need help to organise a summer carnival or prepare press releases. Contact individual charities or offer your services through a volunteers' agency.

'I saw a card in the window of my local charity volunteers agency asking for somebody to give four hours a week to help prepare press and publicity material. I worked with another volunteer who was a PR professional. She taught me an awful lot – how to put together an effective press release, how to use the phone and get past the receptionist – it was invaluable training. She also gave me the names of some other people in the industry and told me to contact them – and that's how I got my first job.'

Account executive, PR consultancy

FINDING THE VACANCIES

The IPD survey on recruitment states that, across all industries:

- 85% of recruiters use the press and specialist journals to contact potential applicants
- 83% use local and 72% use national newspapers
- 65% use employment agencies
- 62% receive speculative applications
- 59% use 'word-of-mouth' contacts.

Use of the Internet is growing all the time. This is rapidly becoming one of the cheapest, most accessible and easiest ways of finding out what jobs are available.

It is likely that in smaller advertising, marketing and PR agencies and consultancies word-of-mouth counts for a far larger percentage of vacancies filled. Recruiting via advertisements, submitted applications and interviews is a lengthy and costly process. In a relatively small professional world, it is more likely that names will be passed from one company to another when somebody is looking for a job or seeking a new employee. However, it is worth looking at all the different ways in which you can access vacancies.

The press

National newspapers advertise a range of vacancies at different levels. *The Guardian* offers the most comprehensive range in its media supplements, which are published every Monday. This should be regular reading for anyone who aspires to a career in advertising, marketing and PR since it will not only offer you leads on jobs but also keep you updated on trends in the industry.

Regional newspapers are useful because many smaller companies will use them to advertise for locally based staff. Occasionally, you may come across vacancies for account management or creative posts. More frequently, you will find ads for clerical and administrative staff and for advertising sales. Don't write these off automatically, even if you aspire to be the managing director of Wily, Wriggle and Wannabe. Everybody has to start somewhere and learning about the commercial and administrative side of a business will give you a firm grounding in how it operates.

If you are seriously pursuing a career in advertising, marketing or PR then you should be reading the relevant trade press. Place a regular order for one of the journals that serves the career area you want to enter and make sure you read the editorials and news sections as well as scanning the recruitment ads. These are fast-moving industries and you need to be aware of current thinking and trends; the trade press will keep you up to date and familiarise you with the culture of your chosen career.

If nothing else, read the ads for fun. No self-respecting advertising, marketing or PR agency would be content with a simple 'we wish to recruit' ad. Many of their offerings in the press are works of art in themselves, as this recruitment ad illustrates:

> ***Recent graduate – fast growing advertising agency***
> *Last time we ran an ad like this, we found Michelle. She's from the north and had about a year's experience working for an agency in Chester. She works hard, cares about her clients and shows the enthusiasm and commitment that differentiate our agency from larger, more established agencies. This week she got a major poster campaign running on the Underground, a £20,000 ad in* The Sunday Times *and she's just been involved in her first pitch for a major blue-chip account. She can also drink several pints of lager without falling over – which is more than can be said for the 30-something blokes who run the place. In return, she's learning heaps and in our view will go far very quickly. Frankly, we love her to bits.*

Newspapers will help you to find agencies that specialise in advertising, marketing and PR jobs. Look for advertisements near the back pages of the *Guardian Media* section. Alternatively, check out the *Yellow Pages* and ring around agencies asking if they offer the sorts of vacancies that you are looking for.

Employment agencies

General recruitment agencies can prove useful if you want to get some basic experience by working in a clerical or administrative position. A period as a temporary secretary, receptionist or accounts administrator could help you to make useful contacts.

At a more senior level, headhunters come into play. These companies are employed by recruiters to target suitable staff. Unlike employment agencies, it is not usual for job hunters to approach headhunters. However, keep your ears to the ground. If you have the right experience and track record and you let it be known that you are thinking of changing jobs, the headhunters will find you.

Speculative and word-of-mouth contacts

Look back at the section on getting work experience (page 59) – the same rules apply for making speculative and word-of-mouth contacts when you are looking for or changing jobs.

When you make a speculative approach, thorough research is essential. Find out about the companies you are approaching – what is their core business, how many staff do they employ and in what capacity, who are their major clients? With larger organisations, ask for a copy of their company brochure or look up their website. Prepare your letters and CVs carefully, so that they 'fit' the company, and make it clear what skills and experience you can offer. Tell the company why you are approaching them. *Never* say that you are sending letters out to other companies at the same time – every employer wants to think that they are special.

You may get a lot of 'thank you for your interest but...' letters. Don't be put off by these rejections; somewhere along the line you will get an invitation to talk to an employer.

Word-of-mouth contacts are used frequently in advertising, marketing and PR, particularly in smaller agencies where ployers do not have the time or resources to go through a lengthy, formal recruitment process. Use your own network and tap into that of your friends. The British are often rather reticent about networking, feeling that it is 'asking for favours'. Put your finer feelings to one side and remember that: (a) networking is an accepted business practice, and (b) most of your friends, relatives and colleagues will want to help you if they can. Tell everyone who will listen what sort of job you are looking for. They may not work in the industry – but they may have a partner/neighbour/brother-in-law who does.

The Internet

The great joy of job seeking on the Internet is that all you have to do is turn on your computer and start surfing. No waiting for publication day and scanning newspapers, no phone calls to agencies. Recruitment ads are posted in their thousands in your own front room.

You can access websites for agencies who specialise in jobs in advertising, marketing and PR. Type *careers + media* into your search facility and see what comes up. Be patient and prepared to wade through a lot of irrelevant material before you find what you want.

Alternatively, look at newspapers on-line. *The Guardian* and *The Daily Telegraph* both have sites that are worth visiting. You can specify the type of job you are looking for, location and even salary range, and you will be shown any appropriate vacancies.

A third option is to look at the websites for professional organisations such as the Institute of Public Relations and the Institute of Practitioners in Advertising. Some (but not all) of these have links to recruitment agencies which advertise on the net.

A word of warning: most advertisements you access through the Internet will be genuine, but do remember that anybody can post information. Exercise a degree of caution and check out any unfamiliar company before you send too many details about yourself. Make sure that the organisation actually exists by asking Directory Enquiries to check the telephone number against the name and address. A quick call to the company will ascertain that they are who they claim to be and that they are recruiting staff. This is not paranoia, it is common sense.

RELEVANT COURSES OF STUDY

People move into advertising, marketing and PR from all walks of life. Your degree could be in any subject from anthropology to zoology; if you have the relevant skills and talents you will still find the job you want.

However, in recent years there has been a rapid growth in courses at all levels that are relevant to different aspects of the communications industry. These range from GNVQs in business studies for those aged 16+, to masters' degrees in marketing. There are too many to list here, but we have supplied contact addresses at the end of this book to put you in touch with organisations that either advise on courses or offer them (see page 93). You will also find it useful to access the websites of individual colleges and universities to get a detailed breakdown of course content.

> 'I have a degree in communications, although that was not directly relevant to PR work. I also did a desktop publishing course that was tremendously useful. More recently, I completed a CAM (Communication, Advertising and Marketing Education Foundation) course that helped to frame PR in the marketing mix, and I would definitely recommend that.'
>
> *Account director, PR agency*

If you are already working in marketing but feel that you lack qualifications, or you want to improve your chances of promotion, you might consider the City and Guilds NVQ in marketing. This is offered in the following occupational areas:

- marketing communications
- advertising
- direct marketing
- marketing products and services
- marketing research.

You will gain nationally recognised qualifications based on practical skills – and you can study while you work.

If you are keen to study a subject that is related to advertising, marketing or PR, choose carefully. Many topics are grouped into diplomas and degrees under the general heading of media and communications. Look closely at any course that interests you and try to make telephone contact with some of the staff who will be teaching the course. Find out exactly what topics you will study and whether it has the focus you want.

'I'm not too interested in what degree an applicant has unless they are coming into the company for a specialised job – I'd expect the company accountant to have relevant qualifications, and all our designers and creative directors have an art school background. But we've had account managers who've studied history, maths, languages, business studies – all sorts of subjects. I don't honestly think studying an industry-related subject at college or university gives you a great advantage. Yes, it's useful to have some understanding of how the industry works, but I'd rather our new staff didn't have too many preconceptions about how things ought to be. In the end, they'll learn as they work and it's their ability to get involved and adapt to the demands of their work that really counts.'

Managing director, communications agency

Graduate traineeships

There was a fascinating 'docusoap' on television a couple of years ago. It showed a group of bright young hopefuls jumping through a variety of assessment centre hoops and being subjected to intensive scrutiny as they fought for a job. The cut-throat competition and the ferocity of the recruitment process made for irresistible – if sometimes gruesome – watching. So, were these young wannabes trying for a place with NASA or the Royal Shakespeare Company? No, they were chasing a graduate traineeship with an advertising agency.

Very few advertising, marketing or PR agencies offer graduate traineeships. Those that do will rarely take on more than a handful of people, but somebody has to succeed and it could be you...

A graduate traineeship with one of the big names will offer first-class training and may give you the chance to cut your teeth on some big-name accounts. You will be working with experts in their field, and stating on your CV that you started your career with Leo Burnett, McCann-Erickson or BBH will give you tremendous kudos as you move up the career ladder.

Many agencies start their graduate recruitment process in October, so you should be making approaches from the beginning of your final year of study. Some companies will recruit via university careers services and the milk round. Others place advertisements for vacancies on their websites. This is yet another occasion when you need to spend a couple of hours surfing the Internet and accessing the websites of companies in which you are interested. Anticipate a rigorous recruitment process from the initial application form through to a place at an assessment centre.

Training for graduates will depend on the structure the agency has in place. You will get 'on-the-job' training where you get practical experience of working on live accounts. You may also be offered external study courses that lead to professional qualifications.

Salaries for graduate trainees with even the largest advertising and marketing agencies are not particularly high. In 1999, London agencies were averaging £15,000–£16,000 and provincial agencies £10,000–£12,000. That's not a lot of money to live on if you work in Central London. Neither is it particularly attractive when you consider the calibre of recruits they expect to attract and the going rate for graduate trainees in areas such as retailing and banking. However, if you are seriously considering a career in advertising, marketing or PR, money will be the least of your concerns in the early stages of your career.

Recruitment into marketing and PR functions with large organisations is similarly competitive. You may find that you have to apply for a management traineeship and move around a number of functions within the company before you go into the area you want. You will, however, get training that is internationally recognised and can put you on the fast track for promotion. You may also be given the opportunity to gain professional qualifications at your employer's expense.

Case Study

Graduate trainee, advertising agency

I graduated in politics and spent the best part of a year trying to get into advertising. I knew that was what I wanted – partly because I'd done some promotions work at the students' union and really enjoyed it, and partly because it offers a fast track career if you can prove yourself.

I applied for a number of graduate traineeships in London but didn't get past the first interview. It was really hard work just filling in the application forms – you could spend days preparing your CV, covering letter and answering the questions they set you. One of the big-name agencies asked me to send in a visual simile of myself and it took me a week to work out what they meant. Another asked: if you were an item in a supermarket, what would you be and why? Some of the questions seemed ludicrous, but I guess they do weed out those applicants who are not really serious about getting into the industry.

I had five interviews with London agencies. Some were very welcoming and informal and I felt that they were really interested in me. Others were very cold and professional – a bit off putting. While I was still applying for jobs, I had a three-month placement with a small agency in Edinburgh. I was the general dogsbody but it was really useful training and I made some good contacts.

How did I get this graduate traineeship? The recruitment ad on the agency's website said that the agency was crying out for fresh blood. I trickled some blood on to a piece of paper (under Sellotape, of course!) and sent it in with a note saying, 'Well, here it is – but it'll be fresher if you see me in person.' It got me a first interview. It's always difficult to know how far you can go to catch an employer's eye. One guy sent in a life-size cardboard cut-out of himself to an agency. He didn't get an interview but I bet he found a job somewhere in the industry. It shows you are creatively minded and on the ball – qualities everybody in advertising has to have.

I rang up the company to confirm my second interview, and they asked me to prepare a presentation. I was given a choice of two topics and chose one about why television was the most powerful advertising medium. I had 24 hours to get it ready so I got some facts and figures together, produced some 3D graphs and slides and I think that swung the interview my way. It was much better than one where a London agency gave me some coloured pencils and paper and 20 minutes to prepare a presentation on 'What is passion?'

As soon as I started here, I was working on my own accounts and seeing through ads for clients. I've started in account handling which is what I want to do, but I'll also spend periods in creative services and sales production. There's plenty of help if you need it but I was working properly from my first day here and I think that's the best way to learn.

The Insider guide to writing effective CVs and completing application forms

Unless you have very powerful contacts or your daddy owns the company, you will have to make a formal application for a job by submitting a CV or completed application form. These, plus your covering letter, are your first point of contact with prospective employers so it is important to get them right. One job advertisement can stimulate hundreds of replies, most of which will be rejected immediately. Employers just don't have the resources to interview everybody who applies to them, so they are ruthless in weeding out any applications that don't meet their selection criteria.

> 'A lot of applicants want to catch your eye and we've all heard stories about unorthodox approaches that worked. But I'm also looking for professionalism in my staff. Any application form, CV or letter that isn't immaculately presented on good-quality paper, correctly spelled and fluently written goes in the bin. That goes for applications that don't come by first class post, too. Gimmicks are fine and they can be fun, but ultimately this is business.'
>
> *Managing director, marketing consultancy*

- Take your time. Application forms demand far more than your name, address and educational qualifications. You may be asked to answer detailed questions, prepare an essay or submit a portfolio of sample work. Request application forms well in advance of any deadlines for submission and start work on them straightaway.
- Follow instructions. If a selector asks for a handwritten covering letter, that is what they want. If they demand details of your previous employment in reverse chronological order, start with your most recent job first. There will always be a reason why a request is made. At this stage, do as you are told.
- Answer questions honestly and get your facts straight. If you make claims that you cannot substantiate, you may get the job but chances are

you won't be able to do it properly. Or, even worse, somebody will expose your claims for the fiction that they are. An application form or CV is a statement of your capabilities, not your wildest dreams.

- Always try to give evidence of your skills and achievements. Tell employers what you have done and can do now, not what you think you can do.
- Don't let a single typo, spelling or grammatical mistake slip through the net. Whether you are going into advertising, marketing or PR, you are moving into the communications industry. You have to be able to communicate 100% accurately. Yes, a lot of the recruitment ads on the Internet look as if they were prepared by copywriters with a literacy age of 11, but that is no excuse for you to make mistakes. Don't rely on software checking programs and do ask somebody you trust to proofread your applications and letters.
- Use good quality writing paper (at least 100 gsm) and a clear printer to create your finished documents.
- Submit your application on time. Keep a record of any correspondence you send in or receive. If you don't hear anything from the recruiter after a couple of weeks, don't be shy about chasing up your application.

What makes a good CV? There are hundreds of books on the market that attempt to answer that question. Most of them reach the same conclusion: a good CV is clear, concise and meets the needs of the person who is going to read it. It should contain two pages of relevant, factual information that summarise your qualifications, skills and experience. By relevant, we mean that your CV should highlight ways in which you can fulfil the requirements of the job for which you are applying.

Don't think you can send the same CV out for every vacancy because you can't. Different employers will be looking for different qualities and skills in their applicants and your CV should reflect their needs.

As your career develops, you may want to explore different styles for your CV. When you first leave college or university, a straight chronological account of your education, work experience, interests and any positions of responsibility will suffice. If you are changing jobs or looking for promotion, you may choose a different format which highlights your past job roles and focuses on your skills and experience.

Preparing a good CV takes time and practice. In the early years of your career, you may struggle to find enough information to fill two pages. As you work up the career ladder, you could find it difficult to decide what to include! Always refer back to the job for which you are applying. If it asks for good communication and teamworking skills and experience of project management, include evidence that you have these abilities.

> 'A lot of people include irrelevant information in their CVs, particularly when they are starting their careers. If I'm looking for a graduate, I don't need to know the grades of their GCSEs and the number of swimming certificates they've gained. What I do want is some indication that they have the skills and experience to do the job. If an applicant is looking for their first job, they may not have direct experience of marketing – but they may have worked on projects at university or college which are relevant, or they may have done the publicity for their student union gigs. That's what I want to know about.'
>
> *Managing director, communications agency*

Look back at the list on page 69. Your CV should be immaculately presented – after all, you're supposed to be a first-rate communicator!

The Insider guide to writing effective covering letters

Every CV and application form needs a covering letter that states clearly why you are getting in touch with the employer. If you are responding to an advertised vacancy, indicate which vacancy you are writing about and where you saw it. Companies may advertise more than one job at the same time to cut advertising costs. 'I am responding to your advertisement in *The Guardian*,' means nothing if the employer has publicised vacancies for an account director, office manager and receptionist on the same day.

You should also give a brief summary of the reasons why you are a good candidate for the job. Highlight any relevant experience, skills or qualifications, but remember that you have dealt with these in more detail in your CV or application form. Finally, invite further contact from the employer in your closing paragraph and let them know if there are any times or dates when you cannot be contacted.

Speculative approaches are common in advertising, marketing and PR. These are industries where unconventional and direct approaches can produce good results. You may hear that a company is expanding and needs more staff or you may want to find a job with a particular company whose reputation you respect. Get a name before you make contact. Nobody is going to be convinced when you write to Fudge, Flannel and Fleece saying how much you've always wanted to work for them if you use the salutation 'Dear Sir or Madam'. If you are genuinely keen to get into a company you will take the trouble to find out the identities of key personnel. Ring up and ask for the name of the managing director in smaller organisations and the HR manager in larger ones, and address your letter to them by name.

MYTHBUSTER

Gimmicks are always a good way to get your application noticed

A clever trick may lead to your application being noticed, but it may not provoke a positive reaction. There is a difference between being witty and relevant and being naff. One of the directors of a marketing agency showed us a flowered, heavily perfumed envelope. It contained an immaculately typed CV and letter, both printed on floral notepaper. And as if that were not crime enough, the letter started: 'Dear Sir or Madam, Do you want an energetic, lively and creative account manager to take your agency into the next century...' Definitely a case for 'file it in the bin'.

The Insider guide to performing well at interviews and assessments

Whether you are applying for a junior's job in a small PR consultancy or a graduate traineeship in marketing with a major retail outlet, you will probably have to attend at least one interview.

Small companies rarely carry out lengthy interviewing procedures. If this is the type of company to which you are applying, you may only be called in once, given a tour of the premises, a chance to talk to some of the staff and less than an hour's questions and answer session with one of the managers. If you are applying to a large organisation, you could go through a process of aptitude tests, preliminary interviews, assessment centres, one-to-one interviews and a couple of days on an Outward Bound course...

Interviews are a two-way process. They help the employer to decide if you are the best person for the job and they help you to make up your mind if this is the company you want to work for. That is the theory. In practice, competition for jobs (particularly at the lower levels) is so fierce that the choice factor is more on the employer's side than yours. It can be unnerving to know that you are up against a lot of good candidates for a very limited number of vacancies but that is the nature of these industries. If you can't face that degree of competition, you are trying to get into the wrong business.

Feeling nervous before an interview is natural and can give you an edge since it may get your adrenalin going and stimulate you to give a good performance. What will help you even more, however, is good preparation before the event. Find out all you can about the job and the company to which you are applying, think about what you want to tell them and how you present yourself. We are taking it for granted that if you seriously want a career in advertising, marketing or PR you will have been studying your preferred industry for some time.

'I loved advertising – it was something that fascinated me. While I was studying for a degree in business studies, I was following the industry in the trade press. When I graduated, I started looking for a traineeship with a major agency. Hundreds of people apply

> but a lot of them don't know why they are applying. You have to really want to get into this industry, and you must do your homework so that you are well informed before you start sending applications in.'
>
> *Associate partner, advertising agency*

People who perform well during interviews have generally spent some time improving their interview skills. This is an area where it is possible to get plenty of help. If you go to pieces at the prospect of an interview, then invest in a couple of good books about interviewing skills or think about attending a course in self-presentation or assertiveness.

Here is a very brief guide to some of the things you should always remember before and during an interview.

- Find out all you can about the company. What do they specialise in? Who are their clients? What do you know about their performance, structure and mission? Larger organisations will have company brochures and other literature that gives you some insight into their operations. Even the smallest company may well have a website. Make sure that you have had a look at these before you turn up for the interview.
- If you have answered an advertisement or been sent for interview by an agency, what do you know about the vacancy? Is there a job specification? If so, how will your skills and experience help you meet the demands of the job? A small organisation may not have a written specification but try to have a preliminary chat over the phone with one of their staff to find out more about the vacancy.
- It is hard to predict what questions you will be asked, particularly in an industry that prides itself on taking novel approaches to standard situations. But it is still worth thinking about how you will answer some very basic questions like why you want this job, what you think you can offer, what you consider to be your strengths and weaknesses. Can you produce evidence

to support any claims you make about what you can do? We can all say that we are great teamworkers or highly creative but how can you prove this to the selector? If you are going for a creative or account handling job and you already work in advertising, marketing or PR, prepare your portfolio in case you are asked to talk about campaigns that you have worked on.

'I had quite a few interviews for advertising jobs. Some interviewers want to see how you react on the spot to difficult questions or situations. I've been given a pencil and told to find three uses for it other than the obvious, and I've been asked which are better – All Saints or the Spice Girls. It's hard because you're geared up for this important interview and you are being asked questions that you sometimes think are pretty stupid, but you still have to come up with an answer.'

Graduate trainee, advertising agency

- Think about the questions you want to ask. Yes, you may be desperate to get the job – any job – but this is your chance to find out all you can about the company. Are you clear about the responsibilities, the assessment and reward structures, the opportunities for training and development? These are all themes that you should explore during an interview.
- Give yourself plenty of time to get to the interview venue and allow for traffic traumas and delays on public transport. They always happen when you need them least.
- However nervous you are, try to communicate some confidence through your body language. Walk and sit with your shoulders back and your head held up. Look at people when you talk to them and they talk to you – and smile.
- Speak clearly – you are applying for a job that is based on effective communication so mumbling, hanging your head and being incoherent will not impress.
- Listen to everything the selector says to you. Answer the questions that they ask, not what you think they

have asked. Take your time and think about your answers. Too many people are afraid of silence and rush to fill every quiet period in a conversation with inane remarks.

- Be honest. Don't make claims about your talents or experience that you cannot support. Somebody, somehow, will reveal the truth!
- Make sure that all your questions are answered and you know what happens next. You should have some idea when and how the company will let you know the result of the interview.

And finally...

What do I wear?

In some agencies and consultancies staff dress very informally. Certainly, in the companies we visited a certain degree of sartorial individuality (and in some cases, flamboyance) was the norm. So what do you wear for the interview? Do you show your sense of style or opt for the conventional?

Play safe. You are dressing for an interview not a chance to show off your fashion awareness. An employer will look at your appearance as a reflection of their company's image; that means your image should be one of professionalism rather than trendiness. Save your style statements for later when you have got the job and established yourself as part of the team.

Above all, check that you are well-groomed, that your clothes are freshly pressed, your shoes polished and your fingernails well-trimmed. Yes, it sounds obvious, but the minor details are often overlooked.

> 'I went to pitch for some business with a marketing consultancy in the north-west. They had a fairly high profile and some impressive clients on their list. As usual, I put on my interview suit. I was ushered into the managing director's office and greeted by this big man wearing ripped denims, clusters of rings and an earring. It was disconcerting but I was relieved that I was dressed smartly. It was his company and he could wear what he pleased but my aim was to convey that I meant business.'
>
> *Freelance copywriter*

Assessment centres

If you apply for a graduate traineeship with a large organisation, you will probably be invited to attend an assessment centre. An assessment centre is not a place but a process that helps selectors to take a detailed look at job candidates. It is a much more thorough way of assessing skills and aptitudes than the standard job interview – and from the candidate's point of view, much more demanding.

Assessment centres vary in format. You may be asked to participate in a one-day session or to spend a couple of days at a residential assessment centre. You will attend along with a number of other candidates for the same job and you will be expected to work together on a range of work-related exercises.

As anybody who has attended an assessment centre will tell you, they can be intense and exhausting. In a short period of time you may have to complete a number of psychometric, numeracy and verbal reasoning tests. You may find yourself role playing in a problem-solving exercise or making shapes out of sticky-backed paper. Everything you say and do will be monitored, often by teams of silent 'watchers' who scribble furiously on clipboards.

If you can enter into the spirit of the assessment centre, it can also be great fun and give you a valuable insight into your own strengths and weaknesses. Here are a few hints to help you cope and make the most of the experience:

- Be willing to take part, even if some of the exercises seem silly. Tests are carefully structured to reveal the information that the selectors require. The assessors know what they are looking for.
- One of the main criteria on which you are assessed will be your success as a team player. Even though you are competing with other candidates on the assessment centre, you will not gain Brownie points by being aggressively competitive or trying to dominate the proceedings.
- Listen, both to instructions and to other members of your group. If you are naturally a confident person,

it is easy to dominate a team exercise. That does not reflect well on your ability to collaborate with others in the workplace.

- Remember that you are being watched all the time. That may include the periods when you are socialising at the end of the day. Getting drunk at dinner will not raise your profile with selectors and having a hangover the next morning will not help you to complete the day's activities. Show some restraint and leave the celebrations until after you get the job.

Making a presentation

If you apply for a job in advertising, marketing or PR, you may well be asked to make a presentation. Presentations and pitches are a standard format for getting new business so most employers will be interested in assessing a potential employee's presentation skills, particularly if they are going to work in account handling.

When you make a presentation, remember the following key points.

- Careful preparation is one of the keys to success. Start thinking about what you want to say well before the interview and put together any visual aids that you want to use.
- Use visual aids when you can – people absorb more information when you appeal to their senses of sight and hearing. You don't need to use state-of-the-art computer technology to prepare a presentation; most PCs have software packages that will prepare overheads. Prepare your materials in advance and test them out. Check with the interviewer that the appropriate technology (screens, projectors, etc.) is available in the interview room.
- Structure your talk clearly – 'tell 'em what you are going to talk about, talk about it and tell 'em what you've told 'em'. In other words, make sure you have a clear introduction, a logical order to the content of your presentation and a summary. Leave time for questions.

- Focus on a subject you know something about because this will make you more comfortable in your delivery. Use notes on memo cards as a prompt but don't read a speech unless you want your audience to fall asleep. Look at your audience and try to maintain eye contact. Speak clearly, maybe a little more slowly than usual, and try to sound genuinely enthusiastic.
- Anecdotes can be interesting but beware of being too personal. Your aim is to show how well you can make a business presentation, not that you have a future in stand-up comedy.
- Practise on long-suffering friends and relatives and, if you can, get somebody to video your performance. You may be surprised to find out how others see you.

GETTING ON

Career advancement can come quickly in advertising, marketing and PR, particularly if you work for a small company; but anyone who wants to get ahead must be prepared to move around. These are not careers where you will gain kudos, responsibility and money according to your age and the number of years you serve with one company.

> 'There is a lot of movement in the industry and it does rather give the impression of constantly revolving doors. It's not quite like that, but staff do tend to change companies fairly frequently. It's an industry where people are hungry and want to progress quickly. The opportunities are there if you look for them.'
>
> *Agency partner, advertising agency*

The culture of these industries offers exciting opportunities and the chance to make it to the top at a relatively young age. However, the degree of flexibility and adaptability that this culture demands is not for everybody. Some people prefer a more formal career structure and to remain in a familiar environment. One major consideration if you are thinking of advertising, marketing or PR is whether you will be willing to change jobs and possibly relocate to advance your career.

As we mentioned before, there is plenty of room for movement between the various functions within advertising, marketing and PR and between the industries themselves.

The following chart shows some of moves made by staff that we talked to. It gives you an idea of how careers can take shape.

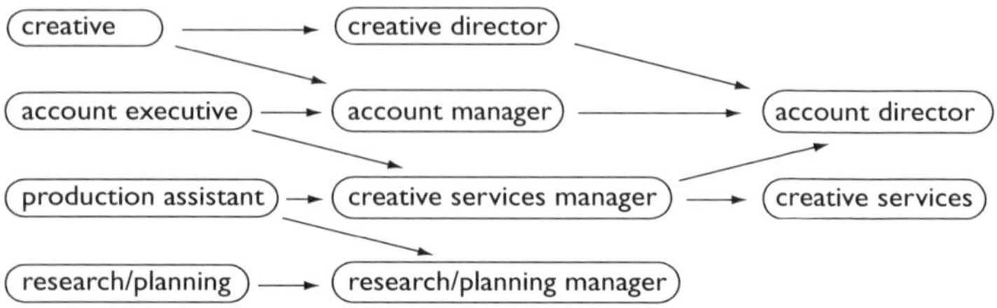

MYTH BUSTER

You'll be on the scrapheap by the time you're 35

There is a tendency to believe that advertising and PR in particular are 'young people's careers'. That's absolute nonsense. If you are a talented creative, an experienced account manager or a PR consultant with a strong track record, it does not matter whether you are 25 or 55. What you may find, however, is that as you get older the physical and psychological demands of the job (long hours, intense pressure, etc.) may take their toll and you decide to move on.

The following comments came from executives in an advertising agency but they apply equally to marketing and PR.

> 'Some departments are more youth-oriented. Historically, creative departments are seen as young and funky – by the age of 30 you'll own your own company or be doing something completely different. That's not so true for the production side, where experience and expertise count for a lot. We tend not to move around so much as the creatives and the people in account handling.'
>
> *Creative services manager, advertising agency*

> 'You can become a senior player in advertising and PR much younger than you can in industries where you have to serve your time. This tends to perpetuate the impression that it's a very youth-oriented industry but there are plenty of executives who've built up long-term careers and are still breaking new ground in their 50s.'
>
> *Agency director, advertising agency*

Professional qualifications

There is no shortage of courses available to those who want to build up their professional qualifications in either marketing or PR. You can choose to follow:

- an S/NVQ course where your success is based on performance in the workplace
- an undergraduate diploma programme, such as the Institute of Public Relations (IPR) course for school leavers, which will help prepare you for a career
- a postgraduate diploma which you can study for part-time and by distance learning
- a postgraduate degree in marketing or business administration.

When you start looking for a course, decide whether there are geographical limitations to where you can study. If you want (or need) to remain in your home town, contact local colleges to see if they have any relevant courses. You could also consider a distance learning course run by a university or accredited college. This will allow you to study in your own time wherever you are.

Bear in mind that these courses are not cheap, so you may need to get sponsorship. If you work in the marketing department of a large organisation or for a large agency, your employers may be willing to sponsor at least part of the course fees. It is always worth asking!

Good sources of information on relevant study courses are the websites of professional bodies such as the IPR and the Chartered Institute of Marketing (CIM). These will help you to identify levels of courses and establishments across the country where you can study. A list of relevant websites appears at the end of this book.

How much will these courses and their related qualifications help your career? That is a difficult question to answer. Certainly, a sound knowledge of the industry, its principles and practices, will give you confidence and may well point you in career directions that you had not previously considered. However, when it comes to gaining a promotion, or joining another company to advance your career, you are more likely to be judged on your practical skills, track record and contacts than your academic qualifications.

GETTING OUT

You've worked in advertising, marketing or PR for a number of years and you've had enough. So, what do you do next? When we asked that question, most of the people we interviewed looked blank, simply because they could not imagine working in any other industry. Moving to another organisation, moving sideways from advertising into marketing or from marketing into PR were good options – but *getting out?* Unthinkable, particularly when people work so hard to get *into* these industries.

But there may come a day when you decide it is time to explore new pastures. Your career will have made you a powerful communicator and this is a strength that you can build on if you decide to move into a different industry.

Account handlers and managers will find their experience of project management useful in many other fields. Bringing together the needs of clients, contractors and in-house staff requires interpersonal and organisational skills that are in heavy demand.

Some areas you might want to explore include:

- event and conference management
- fund-raising and charity work
- e-commerce (a rapidly growing area)
- business management within a professional company such as a law firm or medical practice
- lecturing on vocational courses related to your specialism
- training.

'Fifteen to 20 years is a long time in the communications industry and there can be a degree of burn-out. It's hard work and there's a lot of pressure to meet deadlines and come up with the goods. Some people move on because they want to try something else. They may move into the client field to become marketing managers or directors or they may go into general management. Alternatively, some agency staff become self-employed consultants once they've captured an area of specialism and feel they can make a decent living from it.'

Advertising agency partner

Then, of course, you could always write that best-selling novel based on your agency experiences...

Self-employment

Many people who work in advertising, marketing and PR consider working for themselves. These industries have a degree of flexibility and movement that is unusual even in today's more fluid work culture, and they offer individuals the chance to set up alone with minimal overheads.

Think about it this way: to set up your own market garden, you will need large premises, stock, staff, equipment, transport for your goods and raw materials, storage space and a lot of customers...

If you decide to set up as an independent PR consultant, freelance designer or copywriter, in the early stages all you will need are a computer, telephone, fax, a space at home in which you can work and a couple of regular clients. Unless you tell them, your clients will not know whether you work from your kitchen table or a state-of-the-art-office.

You may decide you want to work for yourself because you are frustrated with your present job, because you don't feel you are moving fast enough or because you think you could do a better job if you were running the show. You may decide to fly solo because you've been made redundant or relocated to another part of the country. You may succeed in establishing a successful practice or you may rapidly discover that the world of self-employment is very demanding and decide to go back into a 'regular' job.

This is not a move to take lightly. If you want to work

for yourself that is fine, but do your homework before you resign from your present job. It is worth sitting down with a piece of paper and carrying out a careful analysis of the pros and cons of self-employment. More importantly, think about your own personality and whether you have the temperament to work alone.

Some of the advantages of working for yourself include:

- autonomy – you are the boss and can decide what jobs you accept or reject
- flexibility to choose your own working pattern
- more varied work if you take on a range of clients
- good daily rates of pay when you are established. You can expect at least £250 a day for freelance copywriting or design and upwards of £350 a day for consultancy
- freedom from commuting! This can give you more time to pursue other interests or spend with your family.

If that all sounds very appealing, don't forget the disadvantages:

- isolation. If you work alone you will not have the feedback and support you can get from office colleagues
- responsibility. The success or failure of a job rests solely on your shoulders. You will also have to do everything, from preparing your VAT accounts to looking for new work
- financial insecurity. You will only earn money when you are actually working and there will be no paid holidays, no subsidised pension fund or company expense account. Add to that the fact that many companies are slow to pay their suppliers. They will pay promptly for the things they need, like stationery and electricity, but can be tardy in settling bills for services such as yours. Your income may become very erratic with thousands coming in one month and then nothing for the next quarter

- endless work. If your business does take off, then forget the idea of self-employment giving you the freedom to enjoy a long weekend in Paris at a moment's notice.

MYTH BUSTER

Self-employment will free you from the nine-to-five

Well, yes, that's true. Instead you will discover the eight-to-11 (that's eight in the morning until 11 at night!). Anyone who is self-employed in advertising, marketing or PR, and is making a success of their business, will tell you about the long hours when the work is coming in. Expect to work through the night and weekend to meet deadlines. During those periods when you are not busy, anticipate sleepless nights and equally fraught weekends as you worry about where your next job will come from.

'I regularly work 70 to 80 hours a week. I get into my office at about 8.30am and never leave before 8pm. Some evenings it's much later or I may have to take visuals to a client. I didn't have a holiday for four years after I started up on my own because in the beginning I was afraid to go away in case I missed some work and later I was just too busy. Gradually I've learned to discipline myself and take at least part of the weekend off, but it's not easy – my office is upstairs and it's too tempting just to go in there and carry on working. Every client wants their job yesterday and if you don't deliver the goods, they'll find somebody who can.'

Freelance designer

If you really have the temperament for self-employment, these words of warning will not deter you. People who work for themselves and succeed will usually tell you that these pressures are nothing compared with the elation and satisfaction you will get from being your own boss.

Here are a few tips for anyone who is thinking of self-employment.

- Talk to people who are already self-employed and find out how they got started.
- Make appointments to see any professionals who can help you, such as bank managers, accountants and development agencies. Explore the possibility of start-up loans or grants by contacting your local council and JobCentre – depending on where you live (or your age) there may be some funding available.
- Make sure you have enough money in the bank to get you through the first six months at least. It will probably take you a minimum of a year to establish a reasonable cash flow.
- When money does come in, put some of it aside for tax and VAT (if you are registered).
- If you are concerned about the isolation of working from home, look around your area for any small business centres or teleworking bases. These will offer you office facilities and a work space for a reasonable rent and you will be working in the same building as other self-employed people.
- Use your contacts. Get in touch with anybody you think could have work for you and make sure they know you are working for yourself. Think about investing some money in your own marketing literature to show samples of the work you do. Be careful, though. If you are resigning a job to go self-employed, check your contract. Some companies include clauses forbidding staff from contacting their clients for a period of time once those staff have left their employment.

Case Study

Managing director, marketing company

When I started out on my own, I wrote to everybody I'd worked with in the past telling them that I was setting up my own business. I took the local paper and wrote to companies where there was a named contact who might be interested in my services. In total, I put out more than 200 letters in two months. Each one included a flier and a business card – people might throw away a letter or leaflet but they tend to hang on to cards.

I also made dozens of follow-up calls. You have to be persistent and refuse to take no for an answer. If I was fobbed off when I tried to speak to somebody, I asked when I could call back and made sure they got a message that I was trying to contact them. I talked to everybody about what I was doing. Word gets around and, in this business, word-of-mouth recommendations are your main source of clients. I'm still getting calls from companies that I contacted during that start-up phase.

There's a difference between being persistent and looking desperate, though. If you chase work too hard it never seems to come in. You have to be positive and make sure that positivity comes through to your clients. If you're not convinced that you will succeed, then you shouldn't be working for yourself.

The hard work paid off and the business has been far more successful than I anticipated. Within three years, we've built up a regular client base of 14 companies and we do repeat work for all of them. That's something else I found important – building up long-term relationships with clients and showing them that you weren't just looking to make a quick buck.

We've made a point of being flexible in the services we offer. If a client wants a service that I can't offer personally, I'm honest about it but I can usually find somebody who can help them. There's no such thing as a job that is too big or too small. I might be organising a regular publication for a company to send to its customers or arranging stationery for a single trader. All jobs are equally important because you never know where they will lead.

The other quality that I think is key to our success is reliability. If I say that I will phone somebody at ten o'clock on Wednesday morning, I phone them. We meet deadlines however difficult that might be. You have to work hard to build up your reputation, and once you are established you work twice as hard again to keep it.

Getting Out brings you to the end of this *Insider Career Guide to Advertising, Marketing and PR*. Now you are ready to start your own research and to apply for the jobs that interest you.

Make no mistake, the competition to get into these industries is intense and you may have to fight hard to get the opening you want. Once you are in, you will face continuous pressure. Jobs in these areas are not for people who want a quiet and settled life.

But if you do succeed, you will have a varied and challenging career. You'll get the chance to work with creative and stimulating people. You could earn a lot of money and travel to some interesting places. Above all, you will probably have a lot of fun.

JARGON BUSTER

Oh, the jargon, the jargon! Well, what can you expect from industries whose primary function is communication? They have both the expertise and the confidence to reinvent the language to suit their own needs – and they often do. Here are some phrases and words that you might come across during your job search. Not only will this *Jargon buster* help you to interpret your colleagues' conversations, it may also prevent you making the unforgivable mistake of using a term that is no longer in vogue. But beware – linguistic fashions change as rapidly as hemlines, so keep checking your language!

Above the line
Sales promotion achieved through expenditure on advertising in the press, on television or in other media.

Account managers/handlers
Liaise with clients and co-ordinate the resources of the agency to produce the required advertising, marketing or PR service. An account director may head a team of account managers.

Ads
You can call them ads, you can call them advertisements. You cannot call them adverts. Don't ask why – just don't.

Below the line
Sales promotions achieved through ways other than advertising, such as reduced price offers, premiums and point-of-sale displays.

Blue-chip company
A well-known and established organisation; usually listed in the FTSE 100.

Brand
A product or service sold under a proprietary or trade mark name. **Brand awareness** is the degree to which people recognise this brand. A **brand manager** is the person responsible for co-ordinating the marketing strategy for this product or service.

Brief
The client's instructions for a project. This could be a vague outline of what they want to achieve or an outline for a specific project.

Cold calling
Approaches made by telephone or in person to potential customers with whom you have had no previous contact.

Creative
The term used to describe the people who develop the words and imagery that communicate a message – copywriters, designers and artists.

Demographics
The study of the statistics of births, deaths and health within a community. This can give valuable insights into lifestyle trends and spending patterns.

Direct mail
Advertising by post.

Direct marketing
Marketing techniques that seek an immediate response from customers by offering them a facility to buy products by phone or mail. Direct marketing may combine various media, such as direct mail, telemarketing, TV and radio promotions.

FMCG
Fast Moving Consumer Goods, such as food, household goods, etc.

Full service agency
As the name suggests, it provides advertisers with a full service to develop advertising campaigns, create individual ads and place them in the media.

Hits
A request for a file on the Internet. Counting these can help advertisers gauge response to Internet advertising. Hits have now been replaced by 'page impressions' as a determiner of traffic. These describe a successful view of a complete page by a web user.

Market position or market share
The position of an organisation in relation to its competitors based on its performance in the marketplace.

Market research
A process of investigating markets for goods and services by examining lifestyle, buying behaviour, etc. Can use qualitative and quantitative data gathered through surveys, focus groups and interviews.

Media buyer
Somebody who specialises in placing advertisements in the media by buying space in publications, airtime on radio and television, etc.

Media independents/specialists
Companies that specialise in media buying. They may also offer media planning and research services.

Media planning
The analysis, identification and negotiation of the media in which a client advertises. This role is becoming ever more important as new media proliferate.

New media
In this book we have used the term primarily to refer to on-line advertising through the Internet. However, cable, satellite and digital television and interactive multimedia can also be included in this classification.

Niche specialists
Advertising, marketing or PR agencies that specialise in a particular type of work such as recruitment marketing, financial PR, fmcg marketing, etc.

Pitch
The presentation an agency or consultancy gives when it is trying to get new business.

Point of sale
A place where goods are shown and sold to customers. Point of sale material is used to stimulate sales and includes posters, dump bins, special displays, etc.

Strap lines
Slogans or phrases that are designed to gain immediate attention.

Traffic
The function within an agency that schedules a project and makes sure each group of people that work on it (i.e. creatives, researchers, creative services, etc.) meet deadlines that have been agreed with the client.

USP
Unique Selling Point. A feature that is unique to a particular product or service and that gives it an advantage over competitors. The usp will be stressed in marketing and advertising campaigns.

WANT TO FIND OUT MORE?

In this section you will find the names and addresses of organisations that can provide more information on advertising, marketing and PR. We have deliberately not included telephone and fax numbers since most organisations prefer preliminary or general enquiries by letter or e-mail. Website addresses are included, and we would encourage you to spend some time having a look at these – you'll find a wealth of industry-related information.

The Advertising Association
The Information Centre
Abford House
15 Wilton Road
London SW1V 1NJ
The professional organisation for those in the advertising industry, it provides a wide range of data, information and insights. You should make every attempt to look at its website on **www.adassoc.org.uk**

Art & Design Admissions Registry (ADAR)
Penn House
9 Broad Street
Hereford HR4 9AP
Application form and handbook can be obtained for admission to colleges offering art, design and media courses.

Association of Graduate Careers Advisory Services (AGCAS)
Prospect House
Booth Street East
Manchester M13 9EP

Produces useful and up-to-date booklets on a range of careers. Ask for its publication on advertising, public relations and direct marketing.

Chartered Institute of Marketing
Moor Hall
Cookham
Maidenhead
Berks SL6 9QH
The world's largest marketing organisation which offers an internationally recognised postgraduate qualification in marketing. There is a very comprehensive website that includes a job search facility on **www.cim.co.uk**

City and Guilds Customer Services Enquiries Unit
1 Giltspur Street
London EC1A 9DD
Provides information about S/NVQs and NEBS management qualifications. It produces a useful handbook. Alternatively, access its website on **www.city-and-guilds.co.uk**

Communication, Advertising and Marketing Education Foundation
Abford House
15 Wilton Road
London SW1V 1NJ
Conducts various education and training programmes. Its website can be found on **www.camfoundation.com**

Institute of Practitioners in Advertising (IPA)
44 Belgrave Square
London SW1X 8QS
It has a comprehensive and informative website at **www.ipa.co.uk**. It includes information on the industry as a whole, careers opportunities, a list of training and academic courses in the UK and links to individual advertising companies' websites. It also publishes a graduate careers brochure which describes the main job functions in advertising. Send a large stamped addressed envelope (at least 60p postage) if you want a copy.

Institute of Public Relations
The Old Trading House
15 Northburgh Street
London EC1V 0PR
Professional organisation which offers membership for people working in PR and offers a range of training courses. It runs a useful website on **www.ipr.org.uk** which offers background on the industry and advice on getting jobs.

Internet Advertising Bureau
No. 1
Canada Square
Canary Wharf
London E14 5DT
The trade association for the rapidly growing Internet advertising industry. Contact it on **www.iabuk.net**

Universities and Colleges Admission Service (UCAS)
Rosehill
New Barn Lane
Cheltenham
Gloucestershire GL52 3LZ
Information about applying for university and college places.

Zenith
The Zenith website on **www.zenithmedia.com** links to many other advertising and marketing agency sites. It also provides a link to **www.revolution.haynet.com** which, at the time of writing, offers an Internet community devoted to marketing and a good job search site.

WANT TO READ ALL ABOUT IT?

There are hundreds of books in print about advertising, marketing and PR. Rather than list dozens of them, we suggest that you look at a good website, such as **www.amazon.co.uk** and browse through its suggestions. This will give you some of the most recent titles, together with a summary of their content.

Directories

There are a number of directories that will give you details of agencies and their work. Look for these in your local library or business resource centre.

Advertisers Annual, published annually by Hollis Directories.

The Advertising Handbook, S. Brierly, Routledge, 1997.

Standard Directory of International Advertisers and Agencies, published annually by National Register Publishing.

Trade Press

BRAD

British Rate and Data, a monthly publication that gives current information on UK advertising media and rates.

Campaign

This advertising industry weekly is essential reading for anybody who's looking for a job. Not only does it contain job advertisements, it provides information on who, where, what and why – essential background on the fast-changing world of agencies. Try the *Campaign* website on **www.campaignlive.co.uk.** Some sections are available only to subscribers, but anybody can take a tour and access job search data.

Marketing Week
The weekly trade magazine of the marketing industry.

Media Week
Weekly trade magazine offering UK and international coverage on all aspects of media.

New Media Age
Trade magazine for anyone involved in new media.

PR Week
The weekly trade magazine of the PR industry.

Newspapers

The Guardian
www.guardian.co.uk

The Daily Telegraph
www.dailytelegraph.co.uk

Notes

Notes

Notes

The Insider Career Guides

Advertising, Marketing and PR
Karen Holmes
ISBN 1 85835 872 8

Banking and the City
Karen Holmes
ISBN 1 85835 583 4

Broadcasting and the Media
Paul Redstone
ISBN 1 85835 867 1

The Environment
Melanie Allen
ISBN 1 85835 588 5

Information and Communications Technology
Jacquetta Megarry
ISBN 1 85835 593 1

Retailing
Liz Edwards
ISBN 1 85835 578 8

Sport
Robin Hardwick
ISBN 1 85835 573 7

Travel and Tourism
Karen France
ISBN 1 85835 598 2

These and other Industrial Society titles are available from all good bookshops or direct from The Industrial Society on telephone 0870 400 1000 (p&p charges apply).